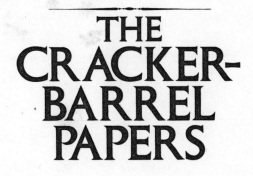

THE CRACKER-BARREL PAPERS

THE CRACKER-BARREL PAPERS

Stan Levitt

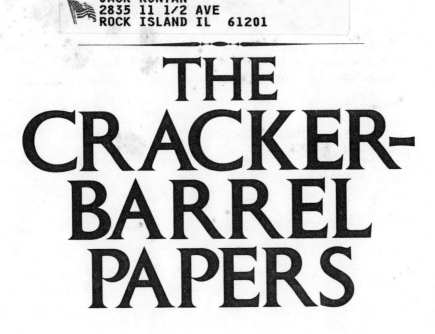

cbi **Contemporary Books, Inc.**
Chicago

Levitt, Stan.
   The cracker-barrel papers, being an account of interesting, lesser-known facts, legends, and truths associated with our great and glorious conflict, the War between the States, 1861-1865.

   Bibliography: p.
   Includes index.
   1. United States—History—Civil War, 1861-1865—Anecdotes. I. Title: The cracker-barrel papers . . .
E655.L48 1977   973.7   77-6912
ISBN 0-8092-7748-4

Published by Contemporary Books, Inc.
180 North Michigan Avenue, Chicago, Illinois 60601
Manufactured in the United States of America
Library of Congress Catalog Card Number: 77-6912
International Standard Book Number: 0-8092-7748-4

Published simultaneously in Canada by
Beaverbooks
953 Dillingham Road
Pickering, Ontario L1W 1Z7
Canada

Contents

Introduction

I was mustered into the ranks of Civil War buffs by the inheritance of an old tintype that had been in the possession of my family ever since Great-Grandpa Herman, splendidly decked out in his new blue uniform, stood at attention before his regiment while the camera recorded his brave image for the ages.

Great-Grandpa's photo was treasured by my family for over one hundred years. I well remember occasions when the tintype was carefully unveiled at family gatherings while eager uncles and cousins vied for position just to touch and view the precious heirloom.

After it had passed from kinsman to kinsman, the great hero's photograph was handed over to its matriarchal keeper, my mother. She then cautiously laid it to rest in a small tin box, and it awaited resurrection at the next meeting of the clan.

When I reached the age of puberty—or during the Lawrence Welk television show, whichever came on first—my mother, in a solemn ceremony, entrusted me with the photograph, first admonishing that great care be taken to protect the family's only claim to historic immortality. Then, with one last gesture, my mother placed her gnarled fingers on the television color dial, turning Lawrence Welk blue, and while the music played the strains of "Tenting Tonight," she placed the old, faded family tintype in my youthful palm.

From that moment on I became mesmerized by any subject remotely associated with the American Civil War.

So avid a collector of Civil War memorabilia did I become that in no time at all my living room took on the appearance of General Grant's field headquarters. Antique Civil War muskets were strategically placed on the walls; old soldiers' canteens and mess kits occupied commanding tabletop positions from every corner of the room.

My wife, who sleeps under a huge portrait of General William Tecumseh Sherman and is flanked on the side of her left toe by a dressing table adorned with hundreds of photos of brave Union soldiers, has for the last five years retired for the evening with the entire Twenty-first Corps.

As a "camp follower," wife and companion, she never failed to put up with all my nonsense. It was at her suggestion that I wrote to Washington, D.C., requesting proudly all information relating to Great-Grandpa Herman's war record. (The National Archives in Washington will supply for the price of one dollar the service record of any Civil War soldier.) Six weeks later I received a photostatic record of my Great-Grandpa's service in the Union army.

Sergeant Herman was mustered in on June 22, 1863, and mustered out July 18, 1863. My illustrious Great-Grandpa served a total of thirty days in the Union army. The way I figured it, he had served just enough time to meet with his fellow soldiers at camp, have his uniform pressed and pose for the damn tintype.

For a dollar my family was wiped out historically.

How could I ever face my relatives and friends with the knowledge of Great-Grandpa Herman's tarnished Civil War record? It has to this day remained my secret.

The pages of this book are the result of notes made from my Civil War readings with the hope that the selected passages would be of interest not only to the scholar but to those who find an interest in historic trivia.

From the beginning I tried to concentrate solely on those authentic bits of history that have borne out the test of years and remain as undisturbed facts. If I have failed in this, my only defense is that I did not knowingly record historical inaccuracies since legends and soldiers' stories do not fade away but have a habit of creeping into historic facts.

I would be sadly lacking in appreciation if I did not mention the many people who, like good scouts, flooded me with the articles found within the pages of this book.

For this kindly assistance I am deeply indebted to James Winter, Dr. David P. Purpora, Joseph Weinstein, Anne Lowell, Gertrude Silver, Dr. Lewis Burrows, Marshal Gartman, Dr. Robert Reiss, Richard Jahn, Robert Jahn, Bessie Berkenholz, Juan Caban, George Suski, Morton Rubinstein, Dorothy Ryan Levine, Ruth Milstein, Ted Kurtz, and Irwin Birnbaum.

THE
CRACKER-
BARREL
PAPERS

I

"The Prince of Ugly Fellows"

All Presidents have received their share of "crackpot" letters, and Abraham Lincoln was no exception. Between November of 1860 and Inauguration Day of March 4, 1861, the President-elect received correspondence from Americans expressing their good wishes for a successful term of office. Not all the letters he received were of a friendly nature, however; some were poison-pen letters filled with the anxieties and tensions of individuals who were quite mad.

Lincoln was about to burn these letters before leaving Springfield for Washington when a friend asked to have them. He obliged; and since these letters were saved from the fire, they were always referred to as the "Hot Stove Letters." Here, then, are several of these "Hot Stove Letters" reprinted in their entirety:

Fillmore La November 25th, 1860

Old Abe Lincoln

God damn your god damned old Hellfired god damned soul to hell god damn you and goddam your god damned family's god damned hellfired god damned soul to hell and god damnation god

1

damn them and god damn your god damn friends to hell god damn
their god damn souls to damnation god damn them and god dam
their god damn families to eternal god damnation god damn souls to
hell god damn them and God Almighty God damn Old Hamlin to
hell God damn his God damned soul all over everywhere double
damn his God damned soul to hell

Now you God damned old Abolition son of a bitch God damn you
I want you to send me God damn you about one dozen offices Good
God Almighty God damn your God damned soul and three or four
pretty Gals God damn you

And by so doing God damn you you

Will Oblige

Pete Muggins

Deformed Sir, The Ugly Club, in full meeting, have elected you an
Honorary Member of the Hard-Favored Fraternity.—Prince Harry
was lean, Falstaff was fat, Thersites was hunchbacked, and Slawken-
bergus was renowned for the eminent miscalculation which Nature
had made in the length of his nose; but it remained for you to unite
all species of deformity, and stand forth in Prince of Ugly Fellows. In
the bonds of Ugliness—Hinchaway Beeswax, President. Eagle-Eyed
Carbuncle, Secretary of the Ugly Club.

Abraham Lincoln Esq

Sir

You will be shot on the 4th of March 1861 by a Louisiana Creole
we are decided and our aim is sure.

A young Creole.

BEWARE

Washington. D.C.
November 24, 1860

Dear Sir.

Caeser had his Brutus! Charles the First his Cromwell and the
President may profit by their example.

From one of a sworn Band of 10 who have resolved to shoot you from the south side of the Avenue in the inaugural procession—on the 4th of March 1861.

Vindex

Sir,

This is to inform you that there is a club of 100 young men in this place who have sworn to murder you.

Jos Bradley
Jos Roints
Mike O'Brien

Hopkinton, Jan 29, 1861

Sir,

Please excuse me for troubling you, but to be short, I want to know if a machine that will fire four or five hundred balls in a minute would be worth any thing, if it is, I have it.

Will you please give me your opinion.

Gilman C. Morgan
Hopkinton
New Hampshire.

A. Lincoln

Grand Meadow Jan 26/61

Mr. A. Lincoln

Dear Sir permit me to introduce myself to you in this letter I am a man that has had the misfortune to mortgage my house and cannot Rase the money to pay for it the mortgage & interest amounts to Seveny Six Dollars Now if you will give me that amount of money you will Be well paid it will save my home the mortg was for the Entrance Monies if you send me $76 God noes you will get it Back agane as soon as I can Earn it if you send it to me you are trusting a stranger But you will never loose anything by it. answer my letter wheather you send the money or not

Youres truley
Ashahel Green
Grand Meadow
Mower Co. Minnesata

Rockford Ills
Jan, 29/61

To Mr.
    Abraham Lincoln Esq.
      Dr. Sir,

I take the Liberty to adress A few lines to you. perhaps you May be surprised at my doing so. but I trust that if your patience will allow you to peruse my somewhat lenghty letter, that you will forgive my presumpsion. My name is Josiah Bowles, and I live three miles west of Rockford Winebago, Co Ills. Well I have been in this country ten years, and the most part of that time I have been Engaged in Horse Stealing and Robbery and Counterfeiting. Now do not start and throw this paper into the fire, but hear me out. Now sir perhaps you are aware that there has been an Organnised band of such characters in this state for the Last ten or fiveteen years. well I am a member of that Band I was sent to Alton Penetentury for one year. In the year 1852, I staid my time out and Lost my Citizenship. Now sir I just have been reading the History of your life, and believeing you to be a man that will do as you agree to, and also haveing the power, I wish to make the following proposition to you. On the 29, of Last March at Ottumwa, Iowa, Mapelo co, One Lunt McCombe Murdered Laura Harvey, and George Lawrence, who left this place (Rockford) on the 16 of last March, in Company with said Lunt Mc Combe. well, the Govenerr of Iowa, Mr. Kirkwood, has offered $500.00. . . . Now sir I am willing to inform you where he can be found, and also to give you such information as will enable you to Break up the whole gang, and also to get the persons (if not got) who Robbed the bank of S.S. Phelps and co. at Oquaka Ills, on the 2 of Jan last of $10,000, ten thousand dollars, providing you will endeavour to get my Citizenship restored, and allow me to have one half of the reward, for I have come to the conclusion that sooner or later if I do not quit this life I will gat catched again, and I think that if I can get on the right side of the law again I can keep so My situation, at the present time is not very Agreeable I assure you.

For on one side I am hunted by the law, on the other watched by my comrads. Now if you think curious that I do not go to C.A. Bradley, or Pinkerton of Chicago (who are Detectivs) or to the Sheriff of this country, and make them this offer, I can give you my reasons for not doing so I am afraid to trust them for, I doubt their veracity and truth very much, and they have not the power to get my Cittizenship restored, Now Mr. Lincoln if you will send some man up here to me, who is an Officer, and send me a paper written by yourself that If I do as I have agreed too, that you will help me as I have hereinbefore mentioned and give me one half of the money received by you as rewards for these men you will find that though I am what I am, I can keep my word, with them that keep it with me. If you conclude to do this you can send a man to Rockford, then come three miles west to One Riley Halls, and within Sight of his house, on farther west, about forty rods, there is a little red house on the south side of the road well stop there and inquire for Joe and the folks will tell you where I am, do not ask any questions of the folks, only inquire where Joe is (do not let any person see this letter except your friends) do not let Bradley of Chicago see it. I have to write this with a lead pencil, in an Old Stable if you do not take the matter up, please drop me a line So that I will know that you have got this. Direct your letter to James Logan, Rockford Winebago co Ills, if you send send quick, or write quick

Yours, Respectfully,

Josiah, Bowles

Today's historians and scholars agree that the romance between Abraham Lincoln and Ann Rutledge, long a favorite subject of novels, plays and motion pictures, is a myth. There are no facts to substantiate this sentimental love story.

Only two bits of evidence have been corroborated: first, that Abraham Lincoln knew Ann Rutledge, and second, that he grieved for her when she died.

In the early 1840s, Lincoln was challenged to a duel by James Shields, the Illinois state auditor of accounts, over a newspaper article reputed to have been written by Lincoln. In fact, it was written by Mary Todd, who later became Mrs. Lincoln. The article satirized Shields' mode of dress and his manners.

Delicate handling of the situation by Lincoln's friends avoided a catastrophe that might have resulted in his early demise. They managed to get him to apologize indirectly.

Lincoln married Mary Todd on November 4, 1842, after a shaky courtship marked by a broken engagement in 1841.

For several months after the broken engagement, Lincoln, heart-sick and despondent, was plunged into a deep state of melancholia. A close friend reported that at the time he even contemplated suicide. His brother-in-law, Ninian Edwards, described him as being "crazy as a loon."

It is difficult to picture him as a romantic figure, yet he possessed all the qualities of a devoted and affectionate husband. He even called his wife, Mary, pet names like "Puss," "Child-wife," "Little Woman" and, later, "Mother."

Lincoln was the first President ever to receive a United States patent.

As a young man he devised a method for lifting riverboats over sand bars. He applied for a patent on March 10, 1849, and it was approved and granted on May 22, 1849—patent no. 6,469.

Lincoln's thin, bearded face is familiar to every school-age child, but did you know that he grew his whiskers on the advice of an eleven-year-old girl?

The following letter was sent to Lincoln while he was still clean-shaven and engaged in his campaign for election:

> Westfield, Chatauque Co., N.Y.
> Oct. 15, 1860

Hon A. B. Lincoln
Dear sir,

My father has just come home from the fair and brought home your picture and Mr. Hamlin's. I am a little girl only eleven years old, but want you should be President of the United States very much so I hope you wont think me very bold to write to such a great man as you are. Have you any little girls about as large as I am? If so give them my love and tell her to write to me if you cannot answer this letter. I have got 4 brother's and part of them will vote for you any way and if you will let your whiskers grow I will try and get the rest of them to vote for you. You would look a great deal better for your face is so thin. All the ladies like whiskers and they would tease their husband's to vote for you and then you would be President. My father is going to vote for you and if I was a man I would vote for you that I can. I think that rail fence around your picture makes it look very pretty. I have got a little baby sister. She is nine weeks old and is just cunning as can be. When you direct your letter direct to Grace Bedell Westfield, Chatauque County, New York.

I must not write any more. Answer this letter right off. Good-bye.

Grace Bedell

Lincoln had the opportunity to thank the little girl personally when he journeyed to Washington as the newly elected President, and his train stopped briefly at Westfield. He greeted the crowd assembled at the depot to meet him and, remembering the little girl's letter, asked if she was in the crowd. Immediately she was brought to him, and he kissed her through his new growth of whiskers.

Lincoln was the first President who did not come from any one of the original thirteen states.

Although he won the Presidential election of 1860, Lincoln did not carry the vote in his own home county of Sangamon, Illinois.

The only Northern state Lincoln failed to carry in 1860 was New Jersey (62,000 votes for Douglas, 58,000 for Lincoln).

Lincoln lost the city of New York by a margin of almost two to one (60,000 for Douglas, 32,000 for Lincoln). New York was a Democratic stronghold and violently anti-Republican during the 1860s, in part because of its economic ties to the South. This concern for its investments was reflected in a startling proposition made by the mayor, Fernando Wood. He suggested that the city secede from the state and establish itself as an independent city-state, an idea that has persisted to this day.

———

The First Lady, Mary Todd Lincoln, was by birth, tradition and family background a Southerner. Nevertheless, she was unfailing in her devotion and loyalty to her husband and the Union. Mrs. Lincoln's three half-brothers, one brother and three brothers-in-law were soldiers in the Confederate army. Three of her brothers and one of her brothers-in-law died fighting for the South.

Lincoln's political enemies accused the First Lady of being a Confederate spy. They went so far as to have a Congressional committee investigate the accusations against her.

On the morning the committee convened, an unannounced appearance by the President shocked the assembled committeemen. He made the following statement:

I, Abraham Lincoln, President of the United States, appear of my own volition before this committee of the Senate to say that I, of my own knowledge, know that it is untrue that any of my family hold treasonable communications with the enemy.

Nothing more was discussed, and the committee agreed to discontinue further hearings on the charges.

———

Mary Todd Lincoln was responsible for doing away with the White House outhouse. One of her accomplishments as First Lady in 1861 was the installation of indoor plumbing in the Presidential mansion.

———

Two Presidents with a war between them both suffered great personal tragedies.

On February 20, 1862, twelve-year-old William Wallace Lincoln, third son born to Abraham and Mary Lincoln, died in the White House after a brief illness.

Two years later (April 30, 1864), President Jefferson Davis lost his five-year-old son, who died as a result of a fall from the balcony of the Confederate White House in Richmond, Virginia.

For the Lincolns, the passing of their son Willie added to the anguish of the death of their second son in 1850. Eddie Baker Lincoln had, at the age of four, succumbed to a lingering illness that had lasted almost two months.

After Willie's death, Mary Lincoln, deeply disturbed in both mind and body, turned toward the supernatural and hoped to contact her son in the world beyond through spiritualism. Seated around a huge table in the Red Room, President Lincoln joined hands with the First Lady at the first seance held in the White House.

The first President to issue a proclamation of amnesty was Abraham Lincoln, on December 8, 1863.

Lincoln wrote the preliminary draft of his famous Gettysburg Address in Washington, and the final draft in Gettysburg.

The popularly accepted legend that he wrote his speech on the back of an envelope while on a train to Gettysburg is not supported by any historical evidence.

Absentee ballots were first used in 1864 by soldiers of the Union army during the Presidential election.

Of a total of 150,635 votes cast by soldiers, Abraham Lincoln, Republican, received 116,887, and George Brinton McClellan, Democrat, received 33,748.

The oft-repeated story attributed to President Lincoln that when informed of General Grant's alcoholic sprees he suggested the same brand of whiskey for his other generals is fictitious.

Versions of this same tale date back thousands of years, and each war conveniently brings them up-to-date.

Was Abraham Lincoln Jewish?

In 1865 a prominent and respected rabbi had these words to say to his congregation:

> Brethren, the lamented Abraham Lincoln believed himself to be bone from our bone and flesh from our flesh. He supposed himself to be a descendant of Hebrew parentage. He said so in my presence.

A prediction made in 1861 by an obscure member of the First Baptist Church of Washington proved to be astonishingly accurate.

Objecting to the sale of the church building and property to a theatrical entrepreneur, this lone church member predicted that turning a former house of worship into a theatre would result in tragic and dire consequences for anyone responsible for such a conversion.

The church and property were turned over to John T. Ford on December 10, 1861. The former First Baptist Church became known in Washington as Ford's Theatre.

On December 30, 1862, the entire interior of the theatre was completely destroyed by fire, with the damage estimated at $20,000. Rebuilt and reconstructed, it was two years and four months later the scene of Abraham Lincoln's tragic assassination.

After the assassination, the government purchased the theatre and converted it into a government office building. And so it remained until 1893, when tragedy again struck. The building collapsed, killing twenty-two government employees and injuring sixty-five others.

While the audience was viewing the play *Our American Cousin*, a real-life drama was taking place in box number seven at Ford's Theatre on the evening of April 14, 1865. John Wilkes Booth fired the fatal bullet that ended the life of President Lincoln.

Booth's original plan was not to kill President Lincoln but rather to kidnap and hold him as hostage until an exchange for Confederate prisoners of war could be arranged. Events, however, altered his plans. He did attempt the kidnapping, but then the war ended, and he must have felt the need for more precipitate action. To this day, no one really knows why he shot Lincoln.

Oddly enough, it was not the first time that fate had thrown the two men together. On the evening of November 9, 1863, seated in the same box at the same theatre, Abraham Lincoln enjoyed the performance of the play *The Marble Heart*, starring John Wilkes Booth.

In 1864, on a heavily crowded railroad platform, there stood a young man. As the train slowly began to move, the crowd suddenly pushed forward and the young man fell between the space along the side of the train and the platform. Almost at once a hand shot out and quickly pulled him to safety.

The young man thanked his rescuer and presented his card. The card bore the name of Robert Todd Lincoln, the son of the President of the United States. And who was the man who saved his life? He was the famous actor Edwin Booth, brother of John Wilkes Booth.

John Wilkes Booth was not recognized by theatre critics of 1860 as an accomplished actor. He did, however, excite his audiences by his ability to make staggering leaps and stage acrobatics, particularly during the dueling scenes in his performances of Shakespeare. It was reported that he "made the mistake of training in the gymnasium instead of in the study." A critic for the Baltimore *Sun* nicknamed him "the gymnastic actor."

Despite his lack of ability as an actor, he did achieve some degree of popularity, and in one year earned over $22,000, an unheard-of sum for an actor in those early days.

Before 1865, several unsuccessful attempts were made to assassinate President Lincoln.

July 12, 1864, was a day that might have altered the pages of history had the aim of Confederate sharpshooters been more accurately directed at the tall target standing on the parapet of Fort Stevens.

Lincoln was on that day observing Confederate troop positions from the high wall of one of the defensive forts surrounding Washington. The Confederates were making a last desperate attempt to capture the capital. A man standing alongside Lincoln was struck by a bullet. "Get down, you fool!" a young officer shouted at Lincoln. The President coolly followed the command of the young Union captain. His name was Oliver Wendell Holmes.

And in 1863, Mary Lincoln was out riding in the Presidential carriage when the horses galloped off with the driver's seat, throwing the driver to the ground. The carriage raced on, tossing its lone occupant out upon the rocky surface of the road, causing her to be hospitalized for a severe head injury.

Investigation later revealed that the Presidential carriage had been sabotaged by the removal of the bolts that held the driver's seat to the body of the vehicle.

The attempt had been aimed at the President, but, fortunately, he had not accompanied his wife.

Was Abraham Lincoln a clairvoyant?

Many notable Lincoln biographers have recorded evidence substantiated by reliable witnesses that our sixteenth President may have possessed supernatural powers.

One cannot easily dismiss the reported dreams of Lincoln as illusions of the absurd. They were consistently directed toward the same ultimate conclusion—his assassination.

While in the White House, he told his wife that upon retiring for the evening he dreamed of hearing people sobbing. As the sounds of weeping grew louder, he left his bed and went from room to room but could find no one in sight. Still hearing the strange weeping, he entered the East Room of the White House and there he saw a corpse resting on a catafalque around which soldiers stood at attention. In the room were crowds of mourners. He looked upon the corpse, whose face was covered, and asked of one of the soldier guards, "Who is dead in the White House?" The soldier replied, "The President; he was killed by an assassin." At that moment, the sobbing from the people grew so intense that he awoke from his dream.

On the day of his assassination Lincoln attended a Cabinet meeting and told the men there of a dream he had had the night before. He had had this same dream many times, and it had always been a forerunner of some good news. The dream was of a ship sailing toward him. Later that day, Mrs. Lincoln spoke of her husband's dream and the fact that on this occasion he was fearful of attending the theatre that evening. His mind, she related, was concerned about the future, and he spoke of his belief that he would be assassinated.

Innocent, casual remarks take on significance when viewed in the light of events that took place that fatal day. One such remark was made by Lincoln to Colonel W. H. Crook, his official White House bodyguard, when he told him he had dreamed for three nights of his pending assassination. As Lincoln was leaving for Ford's Theatre, he turned to his bodyguard and said, "Good-bye, Crook." An innocent remark but, as Crook later remembered, never before had the President said "good-bye" when leaving—it had always been "good night." Those last words of Lincoln's haunted Crook for the rest of his life.

The most remarkable of all of Lincoln's omens was reported by one of his personal secretaries, John Hay. Here are Lincoln's words as related by Hay:

It was just after my election in 1860 when the news had been coming in thick and fast and there had been a great "hurrah boys" so that I was well tired out and went home to rest, throwing myself on a lounge in my chamber. Opposite to where I lay there was a bureau with a swinging glass in it and looking in that glass I saw myself reflected at nearly full length but my face, I noticed, had two separate and distinct images, the tip of the nose of one being about three inches from the tip of the other.

I was a little bothered, perhaps startled, and got up and looked in the glass but the illusion vanished. On lying down again, I saw it a second time, plainer, if possible, than before and then I noticed that one of the faces was a little paler, say, five shades than the other.

I got up and the thing melted away, and I went off and in the excitement of the hour forgot all about it, nearly, but not quite, for the thing would come up once in a while and give me a little pang as though something disagreeable had happened. When I got home I told my wife about it and a few days after I tried the experiment again when, sure enough, the thing came back again.

But I never succeeded in bringing the ghost back after that though once I tried very industriously to show it to my wife, who was worried about it somewhat. She thought it a sign that I was to be elected to a second term of office and that the paleness of one of the faces was an omen that I should not see life throughout the last term.

In the aftermath of Lincoln's assassination, some strange and exaggerated stories were told.

The Petersen boardinghouse room where Lincoln died was so small it could barely accommodate the six-foot two-and-a-half-inch bed on which the President drew his last breath; yet an eyewitness claims to have seen no less than eighty-four people in the room at one time.

There were individual reports credited to some twenty-five people, all claiming to have physically assisted in carrying the body of Lincoln from Ford's Theatre to the Petersen house across the street at the very same time. And eight different people claimed to have supported the President's head while the body was being carried on its short journey to the Petersen house.

The boardinghouse room was left a shambles after Lincoln's

body was removed. Strewn about was the medical refuse of eight hours of tireless effort to keep the great President alive.

What would usually have been looked upon as rubbish suddenly became relics of cherished value. The room was transformed into a treasure trove of collectible souvenirs. The discarded mustard plasters that were applied to Lincoln's skin suddenly vanished. His blood-wetted shirt and blood-soaked sheets and towels were divided into small strips and presented to friends by the owners of the boardinghouse.

Found also on the floor of the room were locks of Lincoln's hair which were snipped off by the physicians in order to better tend the fatal wound. These were carefully separated by the doctors, and doled out hair by hair to people who lived in the boardinghouse. Robert Todd Lincoln also got some hair.

Hardly had the mattress grown cold when the entire bed and coverlet disappeared.

A Union private kept as a memento the eyeglasses he picked up from the gutter of Tenth Street. They had fallen from the President's head as he was being carried to the Petersen house.

Nor was the scene of the crime, the Presidential box at Ford's Theatre, free from the hands of scavengers. They scraped off all the colorful wallpaper and left only small strands of threads from the lace curtains that once hung elegantly in the box. A bloodstained program found in the box at the time of the murder turned up in Kansas years after the assassination. The frock coat, overcoat and pants the President wore on that night were given to the White House doorman by Mrs. Lincoln. In 1968 their value as historic relics was placed at $50,000.

After Lincoln died his body was removed from the Petersen house to the second floor of the White House, where an autopsy was performed. Dr. Curtis, the physician who did the autopsy, cut from his shirt the cuffs stained with Lincoln's blood and presented them to his wife as a memento.

Abraham Lincoln was the first President to lie in state in the United States Capitol rotunda (April 19-20, 1865).

So anxious were the American people to express their sorrow over the death of Lincoln that they overturned the tradition of their time and sent great quantities of flowers to cover his coffin. This established the American custom of sending flowers to funerals.

Wednesday, April 26, 1865, marked the surrender of the troops of General Joseph E. Johnston to General Sherman near Durham, North Carolina. It was this surrender, and not Lee's at Appomattox, that marked the true end of the war. More soldiers laid down their arms for Sherman than Grant.

On the same day, another drama unfolded in an old tobacco barn in Virginia, ending in the shooting and death of John Wilkes Booth, the one man who, by his villainous deeds, conspired to lengthen the war.

Boston Corbett is a name lost in the pages of history. However, in the year 1865 he was acclaimed a national hero. Corbett was the Union sergeant who aimed his revolver through the crack in Garret's burning barn in Maryland, shooting Booth in the back of the head—the exact spot where Booth had hit Lincoln. When asked why he had fired against orders, Corbett replied, "God Almighty directed me."

His early background indicated a mental disturbance that led to periods of emotional depression. His wife died in childbirth, and he took to the bottle and became a drunkard, roaming the streets of Boston. His real name was Thomas P. Corbett, but after listening to street evangelists, he chose the Methodist Episcopal faith as his religion and adopted "Boston" as his given name. He devoted his new life to the reformation of lost souls, and preaching became his sole occupation. A fanatic on the subject of salvation, he went home and castrated himself in 1858 to cleanse the impurity from his soul after two streetwalkers propositioned him.

He joined the Union army on April 12, 1861, responding to Lincoln's call for volunteers. He fought well for the Union cause, but his constant preaching to his men became a source of torment, and he was looked upon as a religious fanatic. He was at one time sentenced to death by a court-martial, but was pardoned by Lincoln. Later, in battle, he was captured and sent to Andersonville Prison, where his total belief in God kept him alive. After a prisoner-of-war exchange, he resumed his duties with the army.

Soon he found himself a part of the detachment of soldiers surrounding the barn in which John Wilkes Booth was trapped. After killing Booth he was hailed by the country as a hero and received the sum of $1,653.85 as a reward.

His army experience over, he preached throughout Kansas in 1878, eventually becoming a doorkeeper for the Kansas state legislature. In 1887 he was sent to the Kansas State Asylum for the Insane for firing revolvers in the halls of the state legislature. He escaped from the asylum in 1888 and from that time forward his whereabouts remained a mystery.

Was the man who was shot and killed in the burning tobacco barn in Maryland really John Wilkes Booth?

So far as the government was concerned the case was closed. Proper identification of the body was made by Booth's physician, who confirmed the scar on his neck as having been the result of an early operation for the removal of a tumor. A desk clerk at a hotel Booth frequented identified the tattoo marks "J.W.B." on the dead man's hand. The evidence seemed conclusive.

But as the years slipped by, reporters, lawyers and accredited investigators began to delve into the case more thoroughly. They interrogated the government's star witnesses and came up with conflicting statements. Doubts began to manifest themselves. It became clear that no positive identification had ever been made.

Soon, there were reports that Booth had been seen, living in Canada, Europe or some small hamlet in the United States. In 1925, no less than five reputed skulls of Booth were being exhibited in different carnivals throughout the nation. The circumstances behind his death had become a mysterious legend.

Today in Washington, one still finds the records of the case being carefully sifted for the one positive clue that will put John Wilkes Booth forever to rest.

————

One of the members of the conspiracy to assassinate Abraham Lincoln was Lewis Powell, alias "Payne."

Booth first made his acquaintance in March of 1865. Powell's childlike adoration of the famous actor fitted perfectly into Booth's plans, and Booth at once realized he had found the right man to murder Secretary of State William H. Seward.

Powell was a Confederate deserter, an unintelligent giant of a man and a thug. After his almost successful attack on Seward, he was caught and placed aboard the ironclad ship *Saugus* in chains.

During his incarceration, he was observed by physicians who were puzzled by his strange behavior. He showed no remorse for his act and displayed no emotion. It was as if in his shallow mind he could not comprehend the enormity of his crime.

A man of tremendous strength, he on one occasion tried to commit suicide by butting his head against the iron door of his cell. Observed continuously for thirty-four days, he was never seen eliminating yet remained in perfect health.

For his part in the conspiracy he was hanged in July of 1865, along with three other conspirators. The other four were given jail sentences.

————

July 7, 1865, was a special day in Washington—it was a hanging day.

The execution of the convicted conspirators involved in the assassination of President Lincoln took place in the afternoon. They had been tried and condemned by a military tribunal.

John Wilkes Booth had already been shot and now lay secretly buried under the prison warehouse floor. The nation was ready for the hanging of Lewis Powell, George Atzerodt and David Herold. But the hanging of a woman, Mary Surratt, was the subject that filled the day.

The officer in charge of the hanging detail, Captain Christian Rath, could not persuade the civilian gravediggers to do their job so long as Mary Surratt was one of the condemned. He had to ask for volunteers from the prison military regiment in order to break the ground on that hot July afternoon, and only after a promise that "every man will get a drink of whiskey when the thing is done" did he get assistance.

In the end, the thing was done: she took her place on the gallows and passed into history. But when she was first brought to the prison, she tried to starve herself to death. The prison physician, Dr. Porter, threatened to force feed her unless she took nourishment. She obeyed—kept alive only to die.

Only one of the accused Lincoln conspirators escaped punishment for his crime. He was John H. Surratt, son of Mary Surratt, the owner of the boardinghouse "where the nest was hatched." The amazing story of his escape and capture centers around a two-year search that followed a trail covering over half the globe.

Fleeing first to Quebec, Surratt then boarded a steamer bound for Liverpool, England. From there he made his way to Rome, where he enlisted in the Papal guards under an assumed name. Recognized by a fellow American member of the guard, he was reported to the United States minister in Rome. After much negotiation between the Vatican and the United States government, his arrest was ordered. Placed under arrest, he escaped from his jailers and made his way to Naples and then finally to Alexandria, Egypt.

In Alexandria he was again arrested and turned over to the American authorities for trial in the United States. After sixty-two days the trial ended in a "hung jury" on August 11, 1867, two years after the assassination.

The government never saw fit to bring action for a second trial and so John H. Surratt was a free man.

He tried to earn a living by lecturing about his experiences, but soon despaired and settled down as a clerk in Baltimore. He died in 1916.

After Lincoln's assassination, Washington was a city alive with wild rumors. Unfounded news reports circulated from every corner of the capital city.

Suddenly, from all this chaos and confusion, Edwin M. Stanton emerged to take personal charge of the government's investigation of the murder. The firm hand of Lincoln's secretary of war touched everything, from the pursuit of the assassin to the final trial and hanging of the conspirators.

Stanton personally interviewed scores of suspects and witnesses. He labored with each new thread of evidence, obsessed with weaving Southern leaders into the assassination plot. Was this the performance of a devoted and loyal Cabinet official seeking justice for his fallen leader; or were these the acts of a man afraid that the evidence might bear witness against himself and other high Union officials?

Time will not allow the case against Stanton to be put to rest. A review of the one-hundred-year-old investigative report reveals apparently innocent omissions of facts. But these facts, when pieced together, point to suspicious and questionable motives in Stanton's handling of the case.

If a Congressional committee convened today for the purpose of determining whether others were involved in the conspiracy to murder President Lincoln, it would be faced with these century-old questions:

Why did Stanton neglect to bring charges against John F. Parker, Lincoln's personal bodyguard and the one man who could have prevented the murder, for leaving his assigned post in front of the door leading to the Presidential box? It was through that very door that John Wilkes Booth entered unchallenged to murder the President.

Why did Stanton keep the contents of Booth's diary hidden from the public for two years, and what happened to the eighteen pages missing when it was finally disclosed?

Why did Stanton refuse Lincoln's personal request that a particular member of Stanton's staff of officers, a Major Eckert, accompany him as a bodyguard to Ford's Theatre on the evening of the assassination?

Why did Stanton neglect to guard the road Booth would use in his flight to the South? By four o'clock on the morning of April 15, Booth was already thirty miles outside the city of Washington.

Why did Stanton delay three crucial hours before sending out Booth's name and description to troops guarding the roads?

Why did Stanton fail to investigate the fact that immediately following the assassination all commercial telegraph lines leading out of Washington were grounded for two hours? This left the capital isolated, preventing communication between Washington and the towns along Booth's escape route.

Why did Stanton refuse to court-martial the soldier who killed Booth?

Why did Stanton order all seven male conspirators awaiting trial for the murder to be fitted with specially designed and hooded canvas head bags? These were to be worn at all times, and prevented them from communicating with anyone.

Was Stanton responsible for withholding the petition for mercy which the court judges attached to Mary Surratt's death sentence? President Johnson, after signing her death warrant, claimed he had never seen it.

Why did Stanton fail to investigate information his War Department possessed one month before the assassination, information that clearly pointed out that conspirators were meeting at Mary Surratt's boardinghouse for the purpose of planning the murder of President Lincoln? Early in March, Louis Weichman, a boarder at the Surratt house, revealed to government officials that he believed a plot to assassinate the President was being planned there. Three officials reported receiving the information and passing it on to the War Department, yet no investigation was ever made.

Stanton was a controversial figure, but he was, nevertheless, held in high esteem by the President. Reports of his early life in Ohio indicate severe emotional disturbance evidenced by several incidents reported by his biographers.

As a young man in Columbus, Ohio, he could not accept the sudden death of his landlady's young daughter. With two young friends he went to the cemetery and dug up the body to prove to himself that the girl had not been buried alive.

The death of his own daughter, Lucy, disturbed his mind to the extent that after she had been buried a year he had her body exhumed and placed in a special metal container which he kept in his room for over a year. When his wife died he was finally persuaded to rebury the child along with her mother. Pathetically, he insisted that his wife's burial clothes be tailored by the dressmaker so that she might appear in death exactly as she had on her wedding day.

His brother, Dr. Darwin Stanton, committed suicide after suffering from a fever in 1846. During the funeral, Stanton was so filled with grief that he raced madly from the church into the woods and had to be subdued by his friends. For days afterward he was carefully guarded for fear that he might attempt to kill himself.

Even in death Abraham Lincoln could not find a lasting resting place. Incredible as it may seem, during a thirty-six-year period (1865-1901) his body was moved seventeen times, his coffin opened three times.

On one occasion, in 1876, a plot was conceived by a gang of counterfeiters to steal his body and hold it as hostage in exchange for the release of a master engraver serving a ten-year sentence in the state prison at Joliet. The plot was discovered by government Secret Service agents, but not before the body had actually been removed from its tomb.

More fantastic than the actual attempt to steal the body is the story of the prosecution of the apprehended criminals. In those days

Illinois had no law on its books against grave-robbing, so the criminals were brought to trial on the charge of attempting to steal the coffin, valued at $75. They were convicted and served a year in Joliet Prison.

Eventually, Lincoln's son, Robert Todd Lincoln, decided that his father's body should remain undisturbed for all time. He ordered a steel cage constructed which was placed around the lead coffin. The coffin was then lowered into its tomb, and cement poured over it so that it was cemented ten feet into the ground. This was accomplished on September 26, 1901; but before the coffin was prepared for its final resting place, Leon P. Hopkins, a plumber, cut a small hole in it and officials peered in in order to confirm absolutely the identity of the body. One of those who looked in gave a brief description of what he saw:

> As I came up I saw that top-knot of Mr. Lincoln's. His hair was coarse and thick 'like a horse's,' he used to say, and it stood up high in front. When I saw that I knew that it was Mr. Lincoln. Anyone who had ever seen his pictures would have known it was him. His features had not decayed. His face was dark, very dark and brown. His skin was swarthy in life. He looked just like a statue of himself lying there.

The hole was then sealed up by Mr. Hopkins, the last man to look upon the face of Abraham Lincoln.

Following the harrowing experience of her husband's assassination, Mary Todd Lincoln became completely irrational in matters concerning money.

While it was true that she did have debts, the manner in which she attempted to meet them indicated the workings of a disturbed mind. The former First Lady would visit pawn shops incognito and pawn her jewels and clothing. She would delight in making unnecessary purchases of useless merchandise, much to the distress of her eldest son, Robert. Finally, she became the victim of a fraudulent New York clothing broker who persuaded her to place her White House wardrobe on sale to the general public.

At this point in her life she needed constant attention; therefore,

Robert hired the mother of the actor Eddie Foy to be her nurse and guardian.

In 1875, at Robert's instigation, a sanity hearing was held in Chicago. In less than five hours, Lincoln's widow was arrested, tried and adjudged insane, leading some to believe that the hearing was rigged, perhaps to save embarrassment to her politically ambitious son. No witnesses for the defense were presented by her court-assigned attorney. Damaging testimony was given by a doctor who stated that Mrs. Lincoln had told him an Indian was removing the bones of her face and pulling wires out of her eyes.

While awaiting confinement in a private sanatorium, Mrs. Lincoln attempted suicide. To her dying day she never forgave her son for having her committed to an asylum.

A year later, she was adjudged sane and went to live with her sister in Springfield, Illinois. Confined to a wheelchair, paralyzed and half-blind, she died a lonely woman in a darkened room on Sunday, July 16, 1882.

In 1865 Congress reluctantly voted the widow of Abraham Lincoln one year's Presidential salary, which, after deductions, amounted to about $22,000.

Five years later, on July 14, 1870, Congress, after much debate, voted Mrs. Lincoln an annual pension of $3,000. Finally, in 1882, the year of Mrs. Lincoln's death, this amount was increased to $5,000 annually, along with a gift of $15,000.

Today, living widows of former Presidents receive an annual pension of $20,000 from the government.

The two guests of the Lincolns' who accompanied them to Ford's Theatre that fatal evening also were destined to meet with tragic deaths. Major Henry Reed Rathbone and his fiancée, Miss Clara Harris, married, and several years later he killed both her and himself in an insane rage.

Robert Todd Lincoln, the only son of Mary Todd and Abraham Lincoln to reach adulthood, believed that his presence at White House functions foreshadowed assassinations.

It is not difficult to understand why he repeatedly refused to accept invitations to political functions when the specific events that led to his fear of being present at these gatherings are recalled.

As Secretary of War under James A. Garfield, he witnessed that President's assassination. In 1901, twenty years later, he was present at the assassination of President McKinley.

But his greatest feeling of guilt, guilt that haunted him all his life, started sixteen years before the Garfield shooting, when he was but twenty-one years of age.

Ironically, it was caused by his refusal of another invitation. He firmly believed that had he gone with his parents to Ford's Theatre that fateful night, he would have occupied the vacant chair by the door through which the assassin, John Wilkes Booth, entered.

Robert was resolute in his conviction that had he been present in the Presidential box that night, he would have been able to prevent the murder of his father.

Andrew Johnson, Vice-President under Lincoln in 1865, delivered his inaugural speech as President before both houses of Congress while intoxicated.

In 1872, Victoria Clafin Woodhull ran for President as the candidate of the Equal Rights party. The first woman candidate for President, she opposed Ulysses S. Grant's re-election.

With the assistance of today's modern communication systems, one of the rarest of Civil War relics was recently purchased by Mr. Paul C. Richards, a dealer and collector of Americana.

On June 9, 1974, Boston's educational television station, WGBH, scheduled a television auction. Viewers were to communicate their bids over the telephone directly to the station when the item appeared on the screen. Mr. Richards almost fell out of his chair when the original "wanted" poster for John Wilkes Booth and two other Lincoln assassination conspirators flashed on the screen.

The television auctioneer declared the value of the poster to be $200 and invited bids at that opening price. But Mr. Richards, because of his experience in dealing with such historic items, knew its true value. It was one of the first "broadsides" ever issued with photographs, and photographs were not then adaptable to printing techniques. "Therefore," said Richards, "I knew they had to have affixed to the printed poster actual photographs of the wanted men."

Several other bidders also knew what Richards knew. When the final television bid was accepted by the auctioneer, Mr. Richards had bought this rare Civil War poster, produced in 1865 at a cost of less than $2, for the sum of $8,050.

History paused for a moment in the city of Dallas, Texas, in 1963 and took a one-hundred-year step backward. The assassination of President John F. Kennedy astoundingly parallels the assassination of Abraham Lincoln.

November 22, 1963 *Assassination of* *President John F. Kennedy*	*April 14, 1865* *Assassination of* *President Abraham Lincoln*
Elected to office in 1960	Elected to office in 1860
Shot on a Friday	Shot on a Friday
Shot in the back of the head	Shot in the back of the head
Wife seated at his side	Wife seated at his side
Never regained consciousness	Never regained consciousness
Working on civil rights legislation at the time	Working on civil rights legislation at the time
Succeeded by a Southerner named Johnson	Succeeded by a Southerner named Johnson
Assassin Lee Harvey Oswald killed before he came to trial	Assassin John Wilkes Booth killed before he came to trial
Assassin's name had 15 letters	Assassin's name had 15 letters

Wife lost a son while she was First Lady	Wife lost a son while she was First Lady
Kennedy name has 7 letters	Lincoln name has 7 letters
Lyndon Johnson born in 1908	Andrew Johnson born in 1808
Jack Ruby, who shot Oswald, pleaded insanity	Boston Corbett, who shot Booth, was found to be insane
The assassin Oswald shot Kennedy from a warehouse and hid in a theater	The assassin Booth shot Lincoln in a theater and hid in a warehouse

---

The President of the United States is seated comfortably waiting for the lights to dim and the curtain to rise on the stage of Ford's Theatre in Washington, D.C. The date is April 17, 1975, and the President is Gerald Ford.

President Ford sat within fifty feet of the balcony box where actor John Wilkes Booth fatally wounded Abraham Lincoln on April 14, 1865. For the first time since the assassination of President Lincoln 110 years earlier, a United States President attended a performance of a play at Ford's Theatre.

II

Heroes and Battles, Money and Taxes

For two politically charged days, May 20 and 21, 1856, the abolitionist senator from Massachusetts, Charles Sumner, held the floor of the United States Senate attacking the proud state of South Carolina and the character of its senior senator, Andrew P. Butler:

> Of course he has chosen a mistress to whom he has made his vows, and who though ugly to others, is always lovely to him; though polluted in the sight of the world, is chaste in his sight—I mean the harlot, Slavery. . . .
>
> There was no extravagance of the ancient Parliamentary debate which he [Butler] did not repeat; nor was there any possible deviation from truth which he did not make. But the Senator touches nothing which he does not disfigure with error sometimes of principle, sometimes of fact. . . . He cannot open his mouth but out there flies another blunder. . . .

To a pure-bred Southerner these were words that could not go unavenged. Seated in the gallery of the Senate chamber, fuming at every word of insult and abuse against his state and its senator, was

29

a member of the House of Representatives, Preston S. Brooks, who, as it so happens, was a relative of the abused Senator Butler.

Southern code demanded that Southern honor be defended by the fighting of a duel, but only between gentlemen, and Senator Sumner was no gentleman in the eyes of Representative Brooks. The code required that those below the rank of gentleman receive a horsewhipping or caning.

On May 22, both houses of Congress had adjourned for the day and only a few senators remained at their desks on the Senate floor. Representative Brooks burst into the chamber and, on the floor of the United States Senate, mercilessly beat Senator Sumner over the head with his gutta-percha cane.

He did not stop until the walking stick was in splinters. Senator Sumner lay on the floor bleeding from the head while other senators held back the assaulting Brooks to prevent him from inflicting further wounds with the stub of the cane. Even as they held him, Lawrence M. Keilt, the other senator from South Carolina and a man who desired the beating to continue, cried out, "Let him alone, God damn you!"

Senator Sumner suffered through a long convalescence, and Northern newspapers made much of the attack. Representative Brooks was tried before a House investigating committee which voted 121 to 94 to expel him. However, expulsion required a two-thirds majority, so Brooks retained his seat. He was eventually charged with criminal assault and fined $300 for the attack.

A year later both Brooks and Butler were dead from natural causes.

This incident of physical violence on the floor of the Senate is evidence of the heated passions that kindled one of the most destructive wars in our nation's history.

As the city of Washington awoke on the morning of March 4, 1861, all was in readiness for the scheduled twelve o'clock ceremony that was to take place on the steps of the Capitol. The President-elect, Abraham Lincoln, was to be sworn in as the sixteenth President of the United States.

At about six o'clock in the morning, just six hours before the inauguration was to take place, the United States Senate, after an all-night session, passes a resolution to amend the Constitution of the United States. This amendment prevented Congress from abolishing or interfering with slavery within the states of the Union. It reserved for each state the right to determine the slavery question without interference from the Federal government.

The resolution had already passed the House on February 27, 1861. Time was growing short. Only a few hours were left and the country would have a new executive. The outgoing President, James Buchanan, signed the resolution in one of his last official acts. All that remained to make the proposed proslavery amendment a law of the land was the necessary two-thirds ratification by the states.

The passage of the resolution by the Senate, its signing by President Buchanan, and the swearing-in of the new President all occurred on the same day—March 4, 1861.

Uncontrollable political events were moving with such speed that the necessary ratification by the states was never obtained, and the amendment never became law. One month later, on April 12, 1861, the North and South were at war.

If this amendment had been acted upon earlier when the crucial question of slavery was hotly being debated, who can speculate on what the effect would have been on the thinking of Southern leaders?

Samuel F. B. Morse, the inventor of the telegraph, was so convinced of the eventual separation of the Union that he proposed the American flag actually be divided horizontally into two separate flags.

This was to be accomplished by having the Northern flag composed of a diagonal blue field containing a star for each representative Northern state, and six and a half stripes. The Southern half of the flag would contain the lower part of the blue field and the lower six and a half stripes.

At no time in our country's history were there a greater number of living former Presidents than during the Civil War. There were five in number: Martin Van Buren, Franklin Pierce, Millard Fillmore, James Buchanan and John Tyler.

Not one of these ex-Presidents supported Abraham Lincoln in the Presidential campaign of 1860.

I went to bed that night as usual and slept quite soundly. I awoke in the gray of the morning twilight, and as I lay waiting for the dawn, the long lines of the desired poem began to twine themselves in my mind. Having thought out all the stanzas, I said to myself, I must get up and write these verses down, lest I fall asleep again and forget them. So with a sudden effort, I sprang out of bed and found in the dimness an old stump of a pen which I remembered to have used the day before. I scrawled the verses almost without looking at the paper. I had learned to do this when, on previous occasions, attacks of versification had visited me in the night and I feared to have recourse to a light lest I should wake the baby, who slept near me. I was always obliged to decipher my scrawl before another night should intervene, as it was only legible while the matter was fresh in my mind. At this time, having completed my writing, I returned to bed and fell asleep, saying to myself: "I like this better than most things that I have written."

So wrote Julia Ward Howe in her *Reminiscences, 1819-1899.* The immortal verse she scrawled in the dim light of morning in 1861 was the inspiring "Battle Hymn of the Republic."

The old saying "You can't tell one player from another without a scorecard" might well have applied to the troops of the Civil War.

In the early stages of the war, several units of the newly organized Confederate army wore blue uniforms similar to those of the Union army. This caused a great deal of confusion on the battlefield, as evidenced by the Thirty-third Virginia, a Southern unit garbed in blue uniforms during the Battle of Bull Run. Federal troops had mistaken them for members of their own army and this resulted in the rout and loss of important Union artillery positions.

As the war progressed, the uniform colors of both sides were standardized: blue for the North and gray for the South.

In 1861 it cost the United States government $42 to clothe the average Union infantry private for one year.

Today it costs ten times that amount just to supply a soldier with the basic articles of clothing, and that doesn't include the price of the special-issue combat dress worn in battle areas.

The first major battle of the Civil War took place at Bull Run, July 21, 1861. The battle site was on a small farm owned by one Wilmer McLean.

After the battle, McLean, in order to avoid future destruction from the war's holocaust, moved farther south to a small Virginia village called Appomattox Courthouse. There he built a new home destined to be remembered by history.

It was in the parlor of the McLean house that Lee and Grant met on April 9, 1865, to discuss terms of surrender to end the Civil War.

Thus, both the beginning and end of the war took place on McLean property, and McLean, who tried to avoid the conflicts of battle, found himself a place in history.

Of the infinite number of war stories that flowed from the pens of Civil War veterans, one stands out above the rest for its sheer incredibility and drama.

The incident the story describes took place in 1862. Whether it is fact or fiction no one can now say with certainty, but a detailed account is recorded in a manuscript written by a Confederate army surgeon, Dr. R. A. Lewis.

The story begins with a battle between Confederate and Federal troops at South Mills, Virginia, in February of 1862, and concludes three years later. The action was by no means a major battle, but the opposing forces exchanged heavy artillery and rifle fire and were dug in behind well-concealed wooded fortifications. In no man's land stood a small farm which was being battered by shot and shell. Suddenly along the Federal line of trenches there appeared a woman and her young child running toward the farmhouse while bullets and shells whistled about them. They entered and took refuge inside the house. As the battle reached its height and the firing grew more intense, a young Confederate who had observed them dash for the safety of the house, and who now feared for their lives, dropped his gun and raced toward the house.

Miraculously dodging bullets, he crawled to the door and threw himself inside. He heard the crying of a child and found in a nearby bedroom the little girl sitting at the side of the bed trying to awaken her dead mother. A piece of shell had struck the mother in the face and destroyed her features beyond recognition. Quickly, the soldier gathered the child in his arms and began to race toward his own lines. The Federal troops, acknowledging his heroic deed, withheld their fire until he was safe behind his own lines. The child was at once sent into Confederate territory and placed in the temporary care of a local tavern owner.

When the battle was over, surgeon Lewis walked about the battlefield searching for wounded soldiers. He entered the farmhouse and discovered the body of the woman. Around her neck she wore a locket, which he carefully removed. Upon opening the locket, he found two miniatures etched on ivory. On one side was the picture of a young girl and on the other that of a young man. He could find no identification on her clothing or in her purse.

The regiment buried the mother without ever learning her identity. The question of what to do with the child remained. It was soon learned that she answered to the name of May, but did not know the names of her mother or father.

In one last attempt to identify the child's parents, the regiment placed ads in local newspapers, but met with no success. Although the troops elected to adopt the child, it was decided that in the interest of her welfare she should live with the family of surgeon Lewis in Richmond.

The story now focuses on the soldier, Henry Dixon, who saved the life of the child. After the war, he returned to his home in South Carolina to find that it had been destroyed by Sherman's soldiers during their march through the state. His parents were dead. He made inquiries about his wife and child and discovered that in January of 1862, they had made a trip to Norfolk, about thirty miles from South Mills, to see if they could locate him.

With this information as his only clue, Dixon went to Norfolk. He spent considerable time investigating and searching out any bit of information he could obtain. He soon left Norfolk believing that his wife and child had either died or vanished completely. Disillusioned and heartbroken, he decided to return home but first went to visit Dr. Lewis, who was living in Richmond, to inquire about the welfare of the little girl he had saved.

As he approached Lewis's home, he saw the little girl returning from school. Her features so resembled those of his wife that he began to shake with emotion. Regaining his composure, he entered the house, where Lewis showed him the locket he had removed from the dead woman three years before.

His hands shaking and his eyes filled with tears, Dixon removed the miniatures from their cases. On the backs of the miniatures were inscribed his name and the name of his wife.

Incredible as the story may seem, the little girl he had rescued from that abandoned farmhouse in 1862 was his own daughter.

Throughout the Civil War each side established a different method for the naming of its battles. This resulted in most of them having two names.

The North referred to a battle by the name of the closest stream, river or creek, while the South named its battle after the nearest town.

The Battle of Antietam (Antietam Creek), as it was known in the North, was designated the Battle of Sharpsburg (Sharpsburg, Md.) by the South. The South called the Battle of Bull Run (named by the North for the stream called Bull Run) the Battle of Manassas, after the railroad-junction village of Manassas.

The North named its armies after large rivers (Army of the Potomac), and the South after land (Army of Northern Virginia).

The "northernmost" battle of the Civil War took place in St. Albans, Vermont, on the Canadian-American border, when Confederate raiders, who had been hiding in Canada, shot up the town and robbed the local bank.

The "southernmost" battle reportedly occurred off the coast of Bahia, Brazil. Engaged in this naval conflict was the U.S.S. *Wachusett*, a Federal warship, which captured the Confederate raider *Florida*.

The United States Army Signal Corps was first established during the Civil War. The system of motion telegraphy through the use of signal flags was originated by Albert J. Meyer, who held the commission in the Federal army as chief signal officer. These "talking flags," or "talking torches," as they were called, proved to be so effective a means of military communication that before long, details of men from various regiments were being trained in their use. Thus, the Army Signal Corps was born.

Paper money was first introduced and approved as legal tender in this country on February 25, 1862.

Scarcely had the Civil War gone through its first year when the North was faced with a critical shortage of coin money. Hoarding caused this situation to become so acute that the public accepted postage stamps as a medium of monetary exchange.

In an attempt to alleviate the shortage, local merchants hit upon the idea of issuing their own fractional currency. Each merchant manufactured his own copper "token" coins, which were redeemable at his own establishment.

Besides relieving the coin shortage, these tokens proved to be an excellent advertising medium. Many of them were elaborately and patriotically embossed on one side, while the other never failed to advertise the product and the name and address of the store. There were twelve thousand known varieties of tokens circulated during the 1860s.

One popular restaurateur, who owned the establishment known as Felix's Kosher Dining Saloon, located at 256 Broadway in New York City, produced a token with the word "kosher" spelled out in Hebrew letters. Without having realized what he had done, Felix had created the only "kosher" money ever circulated in the United States.

The famous Civil War battle between the *Monitor* and the *Merrimack* on March 9, 1862, revolutionized the navies of the world. It was history's first naval engagement between two ironclad warships, and marked the end of the era of wooden ships of war.

Ten months later the U.S.S. *Monitor* sank off the coast of Cape Hatteras during a violent storm.

In the fall of 1973 a team of Duke University oceanographers reported that they had located the wreck of the one-hundred-year-old *Monitor* resting under 220 feet of water. To protect the site from looters and commercial salvage attempts, the governor of North Carolina requested that the Federal government declare as a national landmark the ocean area where the remains of the ship are.

It was the first time in United States maritime history that a marine sanctuary was provided for a ship underwater.

The atmosphere in 1862 grew tense in places like Holly Springs, Mississippi, and Paducah, Kentucky, where the most discriminatory American military order ever issued was put into effect.

Known informally as the "Jew Order" and officially as General Order No. 11, it proved to be a nightmare for families in the region who were forced to leave their homes without trial simply because they were Jews.

The object of the order was to prevent the large-scale traffic in illegal trade carried on by profiteering merchants through Federal army lines. Smuggled Southern cotton brought handsome profits in Northern markets, and Northern medicines and munitions were desperately needed by the South. Once gotten safely through army lines, the Northern supplies could be sold for exorbitant prices paid for in Southern gold and silver. Jews were thought to be responsible for most of this illegal trading.

The official records are clear in pointing out that no one class of people can be charged with engaging in this practice. It was open season for many an unscrupulous merchant who, in most cases, was aided by military personnel in obtaining the official passes that enabled him to transport his cargoes through Federal lines. In handling this matter, President Lincoln was faced with the problem of overriding an order issued by one of his most successful commanding generals. He acted quickly and ordered it revoked, but not before some families had been deported.

Here in its entirety is General Order No. 11, just as it was signed by the commander who issued it, Major General U. S. Grant:

General Order   Hdqrs. 13th A.C., Dept. of the Tenn.,
No. 11   Holly Springs, December 17, 1862

The Jews, as a class violating every regulation of trade established by the Treasury Department and also department orders, are hereby expelled from the department within twenty-four hours from the receipt of this order.

Post commanders will see that all of this class of people be furnished passes and required to leave, and any one returning after such notification will be arrested and held in confinement until an opportunity occurs of sending them out as prisoners, unless furnished with permit from headquarters.

No passes will be given these people to visit headquarters for the purpose of making personal application for trade permits.

By order of Maj. Gen. U. S. Grant:

Jno. A. Rawlins
Assistant Adjutant General.

The loyal Union residents of western Virginia seceded from the state of Virginia, and on December 31, 1862, West Virginia became the thirty-fifth state.

Winchester, Virginia, in the Shenandoah Valley, holds a unique position in Civil War history. Control of the town was one of the most sought-after military objectives of the war. It was occupied by Confederate and Federal armies a total of sixteen times.

On the evening of July 13, 1863, the five-floor New York Times Building became a veritable fort. Reporters, engravers and the entire printing staff were poised behind barricaded windows aiming rifles and carbines at the gathering mob in City Hall Park.

It was the scene of the infamous New York City draft riots, which raged for four days, took the lives of over one thousand persons and caused property damage of well over $2 million. The rioters were protesting the nation's first conscription law. Their targets were the wealthy white citizens and poor blacks of the city whom the rioters held responsible for the war.

The mob had already stormed and gutted the nearby pro-Lincoln New York Herald Tribune Building and was now preparing to march on the New York Times Building. The editor of the *Times*, Henry Jarvis Raymond, remained in his office, his hand on the crank of a newly designed machine gun, the Gatling gun. There was another man in that office, Leonard Jerome, a New York financier, who owned an interest in the paper. Jerome, like his partner Raymond, manned a Gatling gun. Both men were determined to protect their property and, if necessary, give up their lives to save it.

As the rioters turned toward the New York Times Building, police reinforcements arrived and beat back the angry mob, leaving in their wake sixty dead and countless injured.

Raymond attained a place in journalistic history as the cofounder and editor of the *New York Times*. Jerome is remembered

as the maternal grandfather of one of the world's greatest states-
men, Sir Winston Churchill.

The Civil War battle of Missionary Ridge parallels the famous
Charge of the Light Brigade in heroism and daring. On November
25, 1863, without direct orders, Union troops displayed a gallantry
unsurpassed in American history.

Confederate troops were formidably entrenched on the summit
of a ridge which rose almost vertically to a height of over five
hundred feet. Below the ridge were lines of Confederate rifle pits.
The position of the Southern troops was so strategically sound that
General Grant and his commanders decided an assault against
such a heavily defended position would be absolute suicide. Orders, however, were given to drive the Confederates from the rifle
pits below the summit and to hold and occupy these pits. The orders were explicit in directing the troops to go no farther than these
pits once they were overrun and occupied.

Over twenty-four thousand troops massed for the attack as the
signal was given to move forward. And move forward they did. The
Confederate troops deserted the pits and started to climb the ridge.
The Union troops, disobeying their orders, went past the rifle pits
and proceeded to climb the ridge after them. The ridge was so
steep that Confederate gunners on the summit could not position
their cannons to fire down against the oncoming Federal soldiers.
They resorted to lighting the fuses of shells and dropping them
over the side of the ridge. But Federal troops reached the top and
drove the Confederates from the summit.

General Grant, stunned by this magnificent charge, attempted to
find out which of his commanders had given the order for the
troops to climb the ridge. After investigation, he learned that they
had received no direct order. Because of their determined drive in
the heat of battle, they had taken it upon themselves to go all the
way, leaving history to record their impossible victory.

The likeness of Santa Claus as we know him today—a fat, jolly, old gentleman with a long, white, flowing beard, dressed in a red suit—was created by the famous Civil War artist Thomas Nast.

Before 1860 there existed no illustrated prototype of an American Santa Claus. Working for *Harper's Weekly*, Nast made a series of war illustrations for its Christmas editions of 1863 and 1864. In his most famous illustration, "Christmas in Camp" (1863), a merry and pudgy Santa is seen visiting soldiers at a Union camp, bringing gifts to the battle-weary men.

To pay for the cost of the Civil War, the first tax on income was established. The bill, signed by President Lincoln on July 1, 1862, approved a 3 percent tax for incomes between $600 and $10,000. A 5 percent tax was levied on any amount above that figure. The tax percentage was increased in 1864.

The method of paying the tax was a relatively simple affair. Essentially, a citizen needed only to swear under oath that his income did not exceed $600 and he was freed from paying the income tax.

In 1863, the new income tax brought in a revenue of $2 million and in 1864, another $20 million; but it was never an effective method of raising money to support a war that cost approximately $2.5 million a day.

The organization set up in 1862 to handle collection of taxes was called the Internal Revenue Bureau. Its original staff consisted of a commissioner and three clerks, who were expected to handle over eight hundred letters daily. One of their first official acts was the creation of the Federal income tax form "1040." As the war progressed and the work of collecting taxes became more refined, the bureau increased its staff to almost four thousand employees. It was declared unconstitutional by the Supreme Court in 1895.

Some of the decisions made by the first bureau are part of our taxing procedure today.

The Confederacy did not adopt an income tax until 1863. Its rate of taxing incomes was 5 percent between $500 and $1,500, and 15 percent over $10,000.

It is an odd political paradox that in order to preserve our Constitution, President Lincoln found it expedient to perform more unconstitutional acts than any President in the history of our nation. He usurped the authority of Congress by executing the following illegal acts.

> Suspending the writ of habeas corpus, thereby making it possible to detain persons on suspicion of treasonable deeds without benefit of trial.
>
> Forbidding the United States Post Office to handle mail deemed by the President's authority alone to be treasonable correspondence.
>
> Proclaiming by Presidential directive a blockade of Southern ports.
>
> Authorizing the payment of $2 million from the United States Treasury funds without Congressional approval.
>
> Arranging for new laws regulating the issuance of passports restricting foreign travel.
>
> Increasing the size of the army and navy without first obtaining the consent of Congress.
>
> Assuming the power to inaugurate new field regulations governing the operation of the United States Army, a right defined by the Constitution as solely under the authority of Congress.

———

It was during a naval battle in Cherbourg, France, that the decision of a five-year-old boy saved the life of a Confederate captain. The incidents surrounding this extraordinary decision relate to one of the most famous naval battles in our Civil War history.

In 1864, the Confederate warship *Alabama* was taking on supplies in Cherbourg when suddenly, outside the harbor in international waters, there appeared the United States ship *Kearsarge*.

The *Alabama*, under the command of Captain Raphael Semmes, was responsible for the destruction of over sixty-nine Federal ships and was one of the most feared raiders in the Confederate navy. Accepting the challenge to come out and fight, *Alabama*, the smaller of the two ships, made ready for battle. Word spread throughout the coastal villages, and people lined the harbor for a grandstand view of the pending naval duel.

Just outside the harbor was a yacht, the *Deerhound*. Its owner, a wealthy Englishman named John Lancaster, was vacationing with his wife, three sons, a daughter and a niece. He realized his ship was in position for a perfect view of the approaching combat, and wanted to take advantage of this once-in-a-lifetime opportunity. However, there was some opposition from his family, and Lancaster was forced to take a vote to decide the question. Should the family miss the chance to get a first-hand view of a life-and-death battle, or go ashore as originally planned and visit the local French church?

The vote was taken and the church won out four to three. However, Lancaster did not count on the determination of his five-year-old son, who persuaded his nine-year-old sister to change her vote. And so the family maneuvered the yacht into a safe viewing position and prepared to make a holiday of the spectacle.

On Sunday morning, June 19, 1864, at 9:45, the *Alabama* and its heroic crew got under way. A French ship in the harbor accompanied the *Alabama* part of the way, then took a safe position out of range of its guns. The *Kearsarge* steadily raced toward the *Alabama*, and the battle was on.

After several hours of heavy cannon fire the *Alabama* was forced to run up the white flag. Captain Semmes was wounded and, realizing his ship was sinking, gave the order to abandon ship.

There was only one lifeboat that had not been hit, and the *Alabama* sent it over the side with badly wounded members of her crew. The *Kearsarge* sent its only two undamaged lifeboats to pick up the others. Men were drowning in the icy waters and each precious minute meant life or death to them. Captain Winslow of the *Kearsarge* spotted the *Deerhound* and immediately requested her aid in picking up survivors. The *Deerhound* launched two of her lifeboats just as the *Alabama* settled into her watery grave. Captain Semmes, true to the tradition of the sea, was the last man to abandon his ship. One of the *Deerhound's* boats picked up the wounded captain and secreted him aboard the yacht.

When the *Deerhound* returned to England, Captain Semmes was still aboard.

During the siege of Petersburg, Confederate fortifications consisted of a series of trenches approximately a hundred and thirty yards from Union lines. The Forty-eighth Pennsylvania, a Federal unit composed of coal miners, suggested digging a tunnel directly beneath these fortifications and placing explosives under Confederate positions. It was a daring idea, and it received the approval of General Grant; so after twenty-eight days of tunneling, four tons of powder were positioned underground.

On July 30, 1864, the charge was detonated. The explosion created a large crater five hundred yards wide in the very heart of Lee's defenses. At the time of the explosion, Union troops were sent forward to break through Confederate defenses. Unfortunately, the troops rushed into the crater to prepare for their final assault. The Confederates rallied their forces and began to slaughter the trapped Union soldiers, who found it impossible to scale the crater walls.

After several hours the Confederates succeeded in preventing a Union breakthrough. The ingenious scheme of the miners went down in history as one of the war's tragic blunders.

John Jordan Crittenden, a politician from Kentucky, had the distinction of being the father of two Civil War generals who served on opposite sides.

One son, Thomas Leonidas Crittenden, was a Union major general who compiled a distinguished war record. The other, George Bibb Crittenden, an 1832 West Point graduate, served as a Confederate brigadier general. He was arrested by his superiors for failure to perform his duties at the Battle of Bills Springs, Kentucky. He ultimately resigned his commission and was later released.

Six United States Presidents were soldiers in the Civil War:

Rutherford B. Hayes
Ulysses Simpson Grant

James A. Garfield
William McKinley
Chester A. Arthur
Benjamin Harrison

The first major war to be extensively photographed was the American Civil War.

Mathew B. Brady took over seven thousand pictures, many of them large-scale action shots; because of these on-the-spot photographs we have an accurate visual image of that war. Brady was the first news photographer in our history.

Lincoln posed for photographs with his generals, his Cabinet, his sons and his secretaries. Yet of all the hundreds of photographs taken of him, not one was ever taken with his wife at his side.

The name Frederick H. Dyer means little to the average American today, yet over a century ago this unusual man undertook a monumental task. His contribution to American history is as important in its way as that of the soldiers in blue and gray who stood in the ranks and faced one another on the battlefields of this land. His achievement—a three-volume publication entitled *A Compendium of the War of the Rebellion*. It is by far the most comprehensive Civil War reference work ever compiled by one author. He worked alone on it, devoting to his writing over forty years of his life.

In July of 1863, when the orphaned Dyer was fourteen years old, he ran away from his guardian and signed up as a drummer boy with Company H, Seventh Connecticut Infantry Regiment of Hartford. Discharged in 1865, he returned to civilian life and became a member of the GAR (Grand Army of the Republic), a Civil War veterans' organization. Shortly afterward, he began to collect data about Civil War and army organizations. His contacts with prominent state officials, individual veterans, and various state and Federal veterans' groups enabled him to acquire a vast store of statistics. His memory was fantastic, and he became a "walking encyclopedia" of Civil War history and statistics.

It was not uncommon for him to appear before an audience of a thousand or more veterans and answer questions put to him about any regiment, battalion, military organization or unit of the army that had served during the four-year struggle. He could identify all battles, and each victory or loss.

After forty years, he had accumulated some 10 million names and dates handwritten on thousands of sheets of paper, all prepared without assistance from associates or researchers.

The idea of putting all this valuable information into a book didn't occur to Dyer until 1908. Then he isolated himself in a dingy room for five years, eating little and sleeping less, sorting out material, writing and rewriting, determined that his compendium would be accurate to the last detail. Dyer was no battlefield hero, but what he accomplished in that small room was true valor above and beyond the call of duty.

When it was finished and finally published it consisted of three parts. The index alone numbers forty-five pages.

Vol. I is 578 pages and discusses the following:

Military numbers and organizations of all Civil War units.

A summary of enlistments and losses of all Civil War units.

All national cemeteries and their locations.

A list of nine hundred Federal regiments that lost fifty or more men in combat.

An alphabetical list of 7,800 persons who led brigades and larger units, along with the commands held by each.

A regimental index listing by state all cavalry, artillery and infantry regiments and giving for each the date of organization, the headquarters to which it was assigned and the date on which it was mustered out of service.

Vol. II is 413 pages and consists of:

A record of Civil War engagements and losses, arranged both chronologically and by state. Engagements listed total over 10,455 and are classified as actions, affairs, assaults, battles, campaigns, captures, combats, engagements, expeditions, occupations, operations, raids, reconnaissances, scouts and sieges.

Vol. III is 759 pages and contains:

"Regimental Histories" of battalions, batteries, regiments and separate companies, which take into account 3,550 units. These histories explain where each unit was organized, when it was mustered into Federal service, the higher headquarters to which it was assigned, areas in which it served, actions in which it participated, changes in its designation and status, the date it was mustered out and the number of officers and men who died from battle wounds and from disease.

In considering the enormity of Dyer's task, one should know that 1,032 reams of paper and 675 pounds of ink were used during its first printing of 4,500 copies; 6,770 feet of leather and 750 yards of cloth were used in the binding.

———

III

The Confederate States
of America
Are Alive and Well

The Confederate States of America are alive and well!

In 1956 a bank in Sweden exchanged a $500 Confederate banknote for its equivalent dollar value in Federal currency.

As late as 1970 the Liberian government reported that Confederate money had been circulating within its borders as legal tender of the United States.

Perpetrators of such a crime should beware lest they find themselves the duped party. Oddly enough, some genuine Confederate bills are worth many times more than their face value because of their rarity.

Two billion dollars in Confederate currency was issued by the Confederate Treasury throughout the four years of the Civil War. It is ironic that many of these early Confederate banknotes were manufactured by Northern printing companies and then smuggled into the South.

Lacking skilled engravers, the South had to rely on its declared enemy, the North, to furnish its treasury with new currency. In most cases these Northern printing houses were sympathetic to the Southern cause and developed a strange rationale for this obvious conflict of loyalty. They regarded the manufacture of currency a neutral government business, and political concerns irrelevant to the printing of money.

A further note of irony can be seen in many of the engraved scenes depicted on Confederate money. They are Northern scenes rather than Southern vignettes. Imagine Southern storekeepers trading in their own currency with pictures of enemy landscapes elaborately portrayed on the face of the banknote!

Northern engravers and printers were enticed by the Southern government to practice their trade in the South. Many accepted and set up establishments in the heart of the Confederacy. Supplies and equipment were smuggled through the blockade, enabling the South eventually to produce to some limited degree a high stan- dard of quality currency.

Perhaps because of past experience in printing money for other revolutionary governments, these printers and engravers de- manded that payment for their services be made in gold and not in the currency of the Confederacy. Until the end of the war, engrav- ers and printers were the privileged few to whom the Confederate government made payments in precious gold.

As the war continued, the Northern blockade became more ef- fective and Northern banknote companies ceased the printing of Confederate money. By this time the Confederate government had begun to rely on foreign printing presses to supplement its supply of currency.

The first issue of Confederate money (March 9, 1861) was valued at ninety-five cents on the dollar backed by gold. By 1863 it had dropped to thirty-three cents, and on April 9, 1865, to one and six-tenths cents.

The last active trading in Confederate notes was on May 1, 1865. By that time, it took twelve hundred dollars to buy what one dollar could buy in 1861.

As the Confederate army faced imminent defeat during the closing years of the war, the value of its money became so inflated that prices became outrageous.

Here are a few examples of food prices that residents of Richmond, Virginia, were expected to pay:

Potatoes	$ 80.	per bushel
Chicken	50.	per hen
Beef	15.	per pound
Bacon	20.	per pound
Butter	20.	per pound
Flour	1,500.	per bushel
Beans	65.	per bushel

Lucy Pickens, wife of the governor of South Carolina, was the only woman whose picture appeared on Confederate money.

John H. Reagan, postmaster general of the Confederacy, was the only member of the Confederate Cabinet to hold his position throughout the entire four-year conflict.

Under his direction, the postal system of the South was the only governmental agency, Northern or Southern, to produce a profit during the Civil War.

The only American postage stamp to honor a living man appeared as a Confederate stamp picturing Jefferson Davis, President of the Confederate States of America.

Ironically, the Southern rallying song "Dixie" had its roots in the North and was based upon a legend which concerned Manhattan.

Written by a Northerner, Daniel Decatur Emmet, in 1859 for a minstrel show, "Dixie" was based on the story of a mythical Manhattan plantation. Dixie was the name of the plantation owner, who was revered by his slaves because he treated them kindly. It was every slave's dream to work on Dixie's plantation. Those slaves who left and moved south remembered him so fondly that his plantation became their ideal. They expressed their hope of returning in song.

What originally began as a Northern song based on a Northern legend and written by a Northerner came to be identified as the rallying song of the South.

Only one United States President served as a member of the permanent Confederate Congress—John Tyler, who was President from 1841 to 1845. He was elected to the Confederate Congress on November 7, 1861, but died on January 18, 1862, before taking his seat.

Nestled away in the state of Missouri is the small county of Callaway. And if by chance you happen to pass through and discover the local inhabitants in the midst of a celebration, it is likely they are commemorating the most extraordinary event in their history. Callaway County holds the unique distinction of being "the most seceded county in the Union."

It seceded from the United States.

It seceded from Missouri.

It seceded from the Confederacy.

It declared itself a separate and independent "kingdom."

And so, once a year, in January, the natives of Callaway County proudly declare themselves the subjects of a short-lived "kingdom."

Shortly after the surrender of Fort Sumter on April 14, 1861,

President Lincoln, acting through intermediaries, offered the command of the Federal army to a colonel with a distinguished thirty-two-year record of service.

The colonel was Robert E. Lee, who chose to remain loyal to his native state of Virginia.

In 1831 Mary Custis became the bride of Robert E. Lee. She was the great-granddaughter of Martha Washington.

When Lee was superintendent of the United States Military Academy, he carried on a brief correspondence with the mother of a failing cadet. Ultimately, in 1854, he was forced to dismiss the cadet from the academy.

The cadet was James McNeill Whistler. The woman with whom Lee corresponded was Whistler's mother, Anna, whose portrait is one of America's most famous paintings.

Technically, Lee is the only American general ever to have lost a war.

Lee was not the highest-ranking Confederate officer during most of his service in the war. Only in its final months, beginning on February 6, 1865, did he attain full official status and overall authority as commander in chief of all Confederate armies. His appointment went against the desires of Jefferson Davis, who did not like or trust him. Davis preferred to appoint friends to high office.

Before February 1865, Samuel Cooper, a full general who saw no active duty, outranked Lee.

General Robert E. Lee: a man without a country.

An astonishing fact, but his United States citizenship was not restored until July 1975.

By Presidential decree immediately after the Civil War ended, Confederate leaders were permitted to have their full citizenship rights restored provided they fulfilled two government require-ments: the signing of an application for a pardon, and the taking of an oath of amnesty.

Hardly had the nation settled down to the ways of peace than General Lee, having signed the surrender papers at Appomattox a few months earlier, forwarded to General Grant his application for a pardon. Several months later Lee learned that he had neglected to sign the all-important oath of amnesty. He appeared before a notary in Lexington, Virginia, signed the oath and forwarded it to Washington. By some bureaucratic foul-up the two required forms never got together—his signed oath of amnesty disappeared shortly after it was sent in in 1865.

For over a century the disappearance of the amnesty document remained a baffling puzzle. No one knew what had become of it or if, in fact, it even existed. The puzzle was finally solved in 1970 when a member of the staff of the National Archives in Washington accidentally discovered it while going through some old military records.

I, Robert E. Lee, of Lexington, Virginia, do solemnly swear, in the presence of Almighty God, that I will henceforth faithfully support, protect and defend the Constitution of the United States, and the Union of the States thereunder, and that I will, in like manner, abide by and faithfully support all laws and proclamations which have been made during the existing rebellion with reference to the emancipation of slaves, so help me God.

R. E. Lee

In 1975, as a Bicentennial gesture, Lee was finally awarded his full citizenship rights.

———

When Lee died in 1870, the coffin that was provided for his

burial was found to be too short, and so the most honored military leader of the Confederacy was buried without his shoes.

The old general's horse still rides the campus grounds.

In 1970, the United Daughters of the Confederacy assembled around a small granite marker on the campus grounds of Washington and Lee University. They were attending the reburial of Traveler, the horse that campaigned with Robert E. Lee throughout the Civil War.

When Lee died in 1870 while serving as president of the university, Traveler followed behind the casket in the funeral procession, with his master's boots reversed in the stirrups.

Traveler lived for another two years and died at the age of fifteen. In 1907 his skeleton was exhumed and put on display in the school's biology department. The campus superstition then arose that if a freshman inscribed his signature on the bones of Traveler, he would be assured of getting passing grades. Ensuing graffiti caused the bones to deteriorate and in 1963 they were placed in storage until reinterment was possible.

When one looks at the odds against the South at the outbreak of the Civil War, it seems incredible that the conflict lasted for four years.

On the eve of the war, the South, aside from having no army or navy and lacking a strong unified central government, was faced with an opponent that had a manpower advantage of almost four to one. The population of the Northern states was approximately 22 million people, while the Southern states had only 9 million, one-third of whom were slaves.

The North had 110,000 manufacturing plants, while the South had only 18,000. The North produced 97 percent of all the firearms in America and it manufactured 96 percent of the nation's railroad equipment. The country's financial resources, private and governmental, were all in the North.

The Battle of New Market, fought on May 15, 1864, best illustrates the indomitable and courageous spirit of the South.

In 1864 the South was beginning to feel the war's drain on its resources and manpower. Encamped on the outskirts of the village of New Market, Virginia, was a Federal force of some 6,500 troops. The opposing Confederate army totaled about 4,500 men. Badly in need of reinforcements, the Confederates called upon the young untrained cadet corps at the nearby school of the Virginia Military Institute. The schoolboys ranged in age from fourteen to eighteen and the total corps numbered about 215 cadets.

In full-dress battle formation, with the VMI cadet corps flag flying, they gallantly took their place alongside veteran troops and charged a hill heavily fortified with Federal guns. They fought magnificently and Union troops were forced to retreat from their positions. The cadets suffered ten dead and forty-seven wounded.

On the fifth of May every year, the cadets of VMI stand at attention while the names of the dead are read from the honor roll. As the names are called, individual cadets in solemn ceremony step out of their regimental ranks and reply: "Dead on the field of honor, sir."

The indomitable spirit of the South in carrying on the war in the face of acute home-front shortages is evidenced by its ingenuity in producing substitutes for basic household commodities.

"Confederate coffee" was made from dried sweet potatoes and burnt peanuts.

Salt was obtained from filtering the dirt of smokehouses.

Plants supplied much of the dye used to color homespun cloth. "Confederate gray" was obtained from myrtle bushes, and the well-known butternut brown color used in the dyeing of the uniforms was obtained from the hulls of walnuts.

Shoes were soled with wood in place of leather.

The drapes that hung majestically from the windows of plantation homes soon became the material for elegant dresses.

The undecorated sides of wallpaper were used to print the news when the paper shortage became acute.

China and glass were replaced by articles made from clay, and gourds served as ladles.

Soap was made from lye and waste grease.

Pulverized charcoal powdered on homemade hog-bristle toothbrushes served as toothpaste.

In a desperate effort to obtain the chemical niter, necessary for the manufacture of gunpowder, the Confederate government appealed directly to the Southern people for help.

One source of the basic ingredient used in the production of niter was human waste. A call went out throughout the South requesting home-front collection of this material.

On October 1, 1863, John Haralson, an agent for the Niter and Mining Bureau of the Confederacy, placed a notice in the local Selma, Georgia, *Sentinel:*

> The ladies of Selma are respectfully requested to preserve all their chamber lye collected about their premises for the purpose of making niter. Wagons with barrels will be sent around for it by the subscriber.
>
> > [signed] Jno Haralson
> > Agent, Niter and Mining Bureau

This ad set off an exchange of humorous poetic replies:

Jno Haralson! Jno Haralson!
    You are a funny creature;
You've given to this cruel war
    A new and useful feature.
You've let us know, while every man
    Is bound to be a fighter,

The women, bless them, can be put
    To making lots of niter.
Jno Haralson! Jno Haralson!
    Where did you get the notion
Of sending barrels round our street
    To fill them with that lotion?
We thought the women did enough
    At sewing shirts and kissing;
But you have put the lovely dears
    To patriotic pissing.
Jno Haralson! Jno Haralson!
    Can't you suggest a neater
And faster method for our folks
    To make up our saltpeter?
Indeed, the thing's so very odd,
    Gunpowderlike and cranky,
That when a lady lifts her skirt
    She shoots a horrid Yankee!

Agent John Haralson could not resist the challenge, and in answer to the above wrote:

The women, bless their dear souls,
    Are every one for war,
To soldier boys they'll give their shoes
    And stockings by the score,
They'll give their jewels all away,
    Their petticoats they'll lower,
They'll have saltpeter or they'll say
    In earnest phrase—"Wet more!"
The women, were it not for them,
    Our country would be lost:
They charm the world, they nerve our hearts
    To fight at every cost.
What care they how our powder's made?
    They'll have it or they'll bore
Through mines or beds in stables laid,
    And, straining, cry "Wet more!"
Women, yes they stoop to conquer
    And keep their virtue pure;
It is no harm to kill a beast
    With chamber lye, I'm sure.

But powder we are bound to have
    And this they've sworn before;
And if the needful thing is scarce,
    They'll "press" it and "Wet more!"

And even after the war was over the fun did not stop. A Yankee
Boston lady, after having read these literary gems, was reported to
have taken her own poetic license:

Jno Haralson! Jno Haralson!
    We read in song and story
That women in all these years
    Have sprinkled fields of glory;
But never was it told before
    That how, midst scenes of slaughter,
Your Southern beauties dried their tears
    And went to making water.

No wonder, Jno, your boys were brave;
    Who would not be a fighter
If every time he shot his gun
    He used his sweetheart's niter?

And, vice versa, what could make
    A Yankee soldier sadder
Than dodging bullets fired from
    A pretty woman's bladder?

They say there was a subtle smell
    That lingered in the powder;
And as the smoke and fire grew thick
    And din of battle louder,
That there was found in this compound
    A serious objection,
That soldiers could not sniff it in
    Without a stiff erection.

———

General Stonewall Jackson was one of the South's most successful generals, and one of its most religious. His deep piety bordered
on fanaticism.

On the eve of battle he would gather his aides together to join him in solemn prayer. He was known to fall to his knees during a battle to ask God's help. His strict devotion was evidenced by his insistence that the Sabbath be kept by his men and aides. He refused even to mail a letter on Sunday. In his military reports he used the word God countless times, and even went so far as to request the Confederate government to cease all mail deliveries on the Sabbath.

One of his officers best summed up the general's piety when he commented, "I do not know whether Jackson is a Christian or not but this I do know, if he decides to go to heaven, all hell won't be able to stop him."

During the Battle of Bull Run, Brigadier General Barnard E. Bee was so impressed by the ability of General Thomas J. Jackson to rally his disorganized Southern troops back into line that he encouraged his own men by shouting, "There is Jackson, standing like a stone wall!"

It was this reported remark that earned Jackson his famous nickname of "Stonewall."

However, there is another, less complimentary version of this battlefield remark which has become obscured in favor of the more popular one. It was reported in the manuscript reminiscences of Colonel J. C. Haskell.

Haskell's version tells of General Bee saying, before his death a few hours after the battle, that Jackson had refused to move his troops and he in outrage reprimanded him for "standing like a stone wall."

It matters not which version is correct, as the accomplishments of Stonewall Jackson throughout the war earned him the respect of military leaders of both sides.

Frank Crawford Armstrong rose to the rank of brigadier general in the Confederate army, yet he took part in the first Battle of Bull Run as an officer on the Union side.

After the battle he resigned his commission and joined the Confederacy, serving under such prominent Southern officers as Forest, Wheeler, Stephen D. Lee and Chalmers.

The Bermuda Confederate Museum, located in St. George's, Bermuda, is the only known foreign museum to pay tribute to the Confederate States of America.

Over a century ago, during the American Civil War, the port of St. George's, one-time capital of the island, made an essential contribution to the economy of the Confederacy. Clipper ships arriving from England would transfer their vital cargoes of manufactured goods and munitions to waiting blockade-running ships in exchange for their cargoes of Southern cotton. These swift blockade runners could easily outdistance the Union warships attempting to bottle up Southern ports. St. George's merchants and seamen reaped enormous profits from these perilous trips.

The Confederacy maintained a headquarters on the island and it is in this building that the museum is presently housed.

Its most unusual exhibit is a mahogany, fourposter bed that belonged to Confederate Major Norman Walker and his wife. Mrs. Walker, a loyal daughter of the South, had only one wish: to see her child born under the flag of the Confederacy.

She got her wish, although her child was registered as having been born in Bermuda. In 1862 she gave birth to a son, and no one can doubt that he was born under the Confederate flag. On the very top of this fourposter bed can be seen the tattered remnants of such a flag, called the Stars and Bars.

After over one hundred years, they still rally 'round the Confederate flag in Brazil, South America.

When the Civil War ended, many Confederate refugees who could not face a future under Yankee domination fled to South America and established a new way of life.

Today, in the small Brazilian town of Americana, northwest of São Paulo, the descendants of those Southern refugees, grand-children and great-grandchildren, still keep alive their cherished Southern heritage by displaying the Confederate flag in their church and at all local celebrations. Although Portuguese is their mother tongue, they speak English among themselves. The Confederate flag also has an honored place in their museum, which is maintained by a community organization known as The American Descendancy Fraternity.

The climate and land are much like those of the Old South, and, like their Southern ancestors, these loyal descendants grow cotton and magnolias.

IV

"A Soldier Has a Hard Life"

A soldier has a hard life and but little consideration."

"I can advise no young man to enter the Army. The same application, the same self-denial, the same endurance, in any other profession, will advance him faster and farther."

The first quote is from a letter penned in 1855, the second from a letter of 1853. These were strange words, indeed, from a man who was to owe his place in history to devoted service in the Army of the Confederate States of America. The man who wrote those letters was General Robert E. Lee.

The Civil War was America's most costly war. Until the Vietnam War, more Americans died in the War Between the States than in all of America's other wars combined.

Beginning with the French and Indian Wars of 1750, and including the Revolutionary War, the Mexican War, World Wars I and II and the Korean War, Americans lost a total of 606,000 men. Yet approximately 618,000 American soldiers died in the

Civil War, the South losing 258,000 men, the North 360,000.

Illustrative of the fierce fighting that took place during the Civil War are the statistics of a reported sixty-three Federal and fifty-two Confederate regiments. A total of over 50 percent of the strength of these regiments was lost in a single battle engagement.

Sickness and disease accounted for almost 400,000 deaths alone. For every man killed in battle, two men died behind the lines from disease or illness.

———

The bloodiest single-day battle of the Civil War occurred on June 3, 1864, at Cold Harbor, Virginia. The opposing generals were Lee and Grant.

Over 7,000 Federal soldiers fell, while the Confederate losses numbered less than 1,500—an approximate total of 8,500 casualties in less than twenty minutes of fighting.

———

The Civil War army regiment that suffered the war's greatest casualties was the Confederate army's Twenty-sixth North Carolina Regiment. Of its total complement of 800 men, the regiment lost 714 at Gettysburg.

———

The "fighting McCooks" of Ohio served the Union above and beyond the call of duty, constituting the largest family unit to fight for the North. The McCook brothers and their sons totaled seventeen men, all of whom served with the Federal forces. Twelve were army officers (six became generals), one was a naval officer, and the others were enlisted men. Four of the officers were killed.

———

At 4:30 A.M. on April 12, 1861, orders were issued to Southern artillery positions by Commanding General Pierre G. T. Beauregard to open fire on Fort Sumter. The nation was divided and the Civil War had begun.

The Federal fort was under the command of Major Robert Anderson. Twenty-three years had passed since he had been an artillery teacher at West Point, where he had selected one of his brightest cadets to join him as assistant instructor. That former pupil was now General Beauregard, his enemy.

In the same fort with Major Anderson was a Union captain by the name of Abner Doubleday, later acclaimed as the originator of baseball.

In the short space of thirty-five days, a major in the Federal army was appointed superintendent of the Military Academy at West Point (January 23, 1861), a post he held for only five days (January 28, 1861). Then he resigned his commission (February 8, 1861), joined the Confederacy, and gave the orders to open fire on Fort Sumter. His name was Pierre Gustave Toutant Beauregard, one of the distinguished generals of the Confederacy.

The graduates of the West Point "Miracle Class" of 1842 had the most successful military record in the history of the academy.

Out of a class of fifty-six students, nine became generals in the Confederate army and thirteen became generals for the Union.

Despite strong Southern ties, a majority of Southern-born officers in the ranks of the Federal army at the outbreak of the Civil War chose to cast their lot with the Union rather than join the Confederate army.

On April 30, 1861, Robert Selden Garnett resigned his commission from the United States Army and on June 6, 1861, he was commissioned a brigadier general in the Confederate army. One month later he was killed at the Battle of Corrick's Ford.

Garnett was the first Confederate general killed in the Civil War.

There is a monument standing in Fetterman, West Virginia, placed there in 1928 to honor the memory of Thornberry Baily Brown, the first Union soldier to die in the Civil War. He was killed by a Confederate picket in Fetterman on May 22, 1861.

Of the almost 2 million Federal soldiers who participated in the Civil War, twenty-five were reported to be ten years of age or younger.

The Union army boasted of a drummer boy by the name of Johnny Clem, who was mustered in at the tender age of eleven.

During the Battle of Chickamauga in 1863, he put aside his drum, joined the battle and shot a Confederate colonel from his horse. He was wounded twice in battle but continued his army career after the war, retiring in 1916 as a major general.

Cited for gallantry in action during the Civil War engagement referred to as the Seven Days Battle of 1862, young Willie Johnson of the Third Vermont Volunteers received the War Department's Medal of Honor. He was twelve years old at the time, the youngest soldier ever to have won the decoration.

J. C. Julius Langbein enlisted as a drummer boy in the Union army at the age of fifteen, but not before his mother obtained a promise from an officer of his regiment to take care of her young soldier son.

On April 19, 1862, drummer boy Langbein, in action at Camden, North Carolina, won the Medal of Honor. A portion of his citation read: "He voluntarily and under heavy fire went to the aid of a wounded officer, procured medical assistance for him and aided in carrying him to a place of safety."

The life of the officer he saved was the very same man who promised Julius' mother to watch over him.

The youngest general officer on either side during the Civil War was Galusha Pennypacker, who was born on June 1, 1844, enlisted at the age of sixteen and became a Union brevet major general at the tender age of twenty.

He was not old enough to vote until the war was over.

In 1862, nineteen-year-old Albert Cashier enlisted in the Federal army as a private in the Ninety-fifth Illinois and served through the campaigns at Vicksburg, Red River and Nashville. After receiving an honorable discharge in 1865, Private Cashier returned to civilian life.

Forty-six years after the war ended, a startling fact was revealed: Veteran soldier Albert Cashier was a woman.

She continued to receive a soldier's pension until her death in 1915.

When Private Budwin enlisted in the Union army, his wife, disguised as a man, enlisted along with him. Serving together, they were both captured and imprisoned at Andersonville Prison.

Mrs. Budwin, continuing her masquerade, suffered along with her fellow male prisoners. Her husband was shot and killed by a guard, and she was transferred to another prison where her sex was discovered by the prison's examining doctor.

She died on January 25, 1865, at the Confederate prison camp located in Florence, South Carolina, just one month before she was to be paroled.

So far as the records indicate, Mrs. Florence Budwin, a private in the Union army, was the only known female prisoner of war confined at Andersonville.

"Old soldiers never die"—and so it was with John Burns (Farmer Burns). Upon hearing the thunder of battle, he could not stay his old soldier's heart from joining the ranks of his comrades just one more time.

He put on his 1812 army uniform, took in hand his old rifle, and became the only citizen of Gettysburg, Pennsylvania, to fight with Union soldiers at the three-day Battle of Gettysburg.

The oldest Yankee Civil War soldier was Curtis King, who at the age of eighty enlisted in the Thirty-seventh Iowa Regiment in 1862.

In the Confederate ranks, the oldest soldier on record was Private F. Pollard of the Fifth North Carolina. He was seventy-three years old at the time of his enlistment in 1862.

The last surviving veteran of the Civil War was Walter Williams, a member of Hoods Brigade of the Confederate army. On December 19, 1959, he died in Houston, Texas, at the age of 117.

The highest rank attained by a private on either side during the Civil War was that of lieutenant general.

Having enlisted in the Seventh Tennessee Cavalry, Private Nathan Bedford Forrest rose rapidly through the Confederate ranks until he was promoted to lieutenant general. He had only six months of formal schooling and no prior military training.

The first man in American naval history to achieve the rank of full admiral was David G. Farragut ("Damn the torpedoes. Full speed ahead!"), hero of the Battle of Mobile Bay, August 5, 1864.

———

Approximately twenty-three hundred Union and six hundred Confederate chaplains served the armed forces during the Civil War. Of these, two from the Union and thirteen from the Confederacy were killed in battle. Three Union chaplains received the Congressional Medal of Honor for bravery under fire.

———

"Go to hell, you damned sons of bitches!" Those were the words that echoed from the lips of a Confederate chaplain.

In the heat of battle, emotions so often take control of reason that even a parson can forget his divine vows. Such was the situation Parson Brady of the Thirteenth Arkansas found himself in. During a battle he forgot his role as chaplain and chased Yankee soldiers from the field. When the toll was taken, it was found that he had shot two Yankees and in hand-to-hand combat had slashed the throat of a third.

———

The records of the Civil War show no officially commissioned chaplains of the Jewish faith in the Confederate army. However, many Southern Jewish soldiers filled in as volunteer rabbis in the field.

———

Loyalty to a cause can sometimes direct the conscience of a man to change from one uniform to another.

Leonidas Polk's transformation was more extreme than most. A graduate of West Point in 1827, he later became an ordained minister and then a bishop of the Protestant Episcopal Church. But he felt allegiance to the Confederate cause, and having been educated as a soldier, changed his Episcopal robes to the uniform of a lieutenant general of the Confederate army.

As a corps commander, he fought at the battles of Belmont, Shiloh, Perrysville and Murfreesboro. He was killed in the fighting at Pine Mountain in June 1865.

In 1854, while serving in a western military post, a young army officer was forced to resign his commission. The charge: intoxicated while on duty.

The resignation was accepted by the then Secretary of War for the United States, Jefferson Davis. The officer involved in the incident was later to become Davis' chief adversary during the Civil War—Ulysses S. Grant.

General Grant's qualities as a "fighting general" were first brought to the attention of the nation and President Lincoln by his successful campaigns against Fort Henry and Fort Donelson on the Cumberland River in Tennessee in 1862.

His terms of "unconditional surrender" at Fort Donelson became so popular in the Northern press that people associated them with the first two initials of his name. He became known as "Unconditional Surrender" Grant.

General Floyd was in command of the Confederate forces at Fort Donelson and did not wish to be captured by Grant. He turned his command over to General Pillow, who refused it. The surrender of Fort Donelson was officially carried out by General Simon Bolivar Buckner while Generals Floyd and Pillow made their escape to Confederate lines. General Buckner was the father of Lieutenant General Buckner of World War II fame.

After Grant's victory a newspaper reporter described him as smoking a cigar even though he had always been a pipe smoker. The general was presented with so many boxes of cigars that he gave up his pipe and became a devoted cigar smoker. He died of cancer of the throat in 1885.

One of the most distinguished soldiers in the Revolutionary War won not only the praise and confidence of General Washington but also a medal from Congress for his skill and daring. The soldier was Major General Henry ("Light Horse Harry") Lee, whose bravery on the battlefield helped forge this country into a united nation.

Eighty-three years later, his son, Robert E. Lee, displayed those same battlefield skills and almost divided that nation.

Confederate private John Rowlands was taken prisoner at the Battle of Shiloh in 1862. As a prisoner of war he took the oath of allegiance to the United States government and joined the Union army. Former Confederates turned Yankee were known as "Galvanized Confederates." A "Galvanized Yankee" was in the reverse situation.

Now wearing a Yankee blue uniform, Rowlands served as a private for a brief period until he received a medical discharge. After a while he again changed uniforms, joining the Union navy, from which he later deserted in 1866.

In the years following the war, Rowlands became world famous as a newspaper reporter for the New York *Herald*. He explored the jungles of Africa and won a place in history for his one sentence greeting: "Dr. Livingston, I presume?" History remembers him by his adopted name, Henry M. Stanley.

There is a footnote to this incredible story that takes us back to the Battle of Gettysburg in 1863. During the battle, a young eighteen-year-old English-born Union soldier was wounded. He was the son of the English missionary explorer Dr. David Livingston.

A young Swiss immigrant by the name of Emil Frey enlisted as a sergeant in Company E of the Twenty-fourth Illinois Regiment on July 8, 1861. On August 29 of that year he was commissioned a second lieutenant. He later became a captain of the Eighty-second Illinois Regiment, eventually rising to the rank of brevet major "for gallant and meritorious service during the war."

What makes Major Frey's story unique is the fact that after the war he returned to his native land, Switzerland, and became president of his country. As far as the records indicate, he is the only Civil War veteran known to have become the head of a foreign nation.

———

Confederate general Joseph E. Johnston ("Uncle Joe") of Virginia, one of the South's more able commanders, was the great-nephew of Patrick Henry.

———

Manning M. Kimmel was a young Union cavalry lieutenant who fought at the opening Battle of Bull Run. Later, he resigned his Union commission and joined the Confederate army to become an assistant adjutant general.

Eighty years later the scene was set for another opening battle. This time the commander was Admiral Husband F. Kimmel, who was in charge of the American naval base at Pearl Harbor on December 7, 1941.

Admiral Kimmel was the son of Confederate general Manning M. Kimmel.

———

Colonel Patton, a daring young Confederate officer who commanded a Virginia brigade, was killed in action during the Battle of Winchester in 1864.

His grandson won fame in World War II as the controversial commander of the United States Third Army, General George S. Patton, Jr.

———

Josiah Gorgas was a graduate of the United States Military Academy in 1841. Resigning his captain's commission at the outbreak of the Civil War, he joined the Confederate army and achieved the rank of brigadier general, chief of Confederate ordnance. Gorgas' son was the famous surgeon William C. Gorgas, the sanitation expert who made it possible to complete the Panama Canal. Because of his efforts to control the mosquito population, further outbreaks of yellow fever were prevented.

Serving with the First Virginia Confederate Cavalry was a private who in 1864 deserted his fellow troopers by riding off into the Virginia sunset never to be heard from again.

The reason for his desertion was never fully explained. However, he certainly was not the most popular soldier in camp.

The name of this Confederate private was Abraham Lincoln.

Union general George Armstrong Custer designed his own uniform and was said to look "like a circus rider gone mad!" Throughout the military history of the United States, he was the only soldier to wear a velvet uniform.

As soon as General Joseph Hooker took command of the Army of the Potomac in January 1863, a more relaxed attitude toward sexual activities existed among the troops under his command.

Camp followers and prostitutes engaged in their trade with utter abandon and without fear of military restrictions. The slang expression "hooker" was said to have been derived from the general's name.

Reposing in the vast files of the National Archives in Washington is a document containing the confession of a camp follower by the name of Annie Jones.

Her most significant revelation was her admission of illicit sexual relationships with two high-ranking Federal Civil War generals, General Kilpatrick and General Custer.

General Custer denounced the charges as untrue. Although he did admit that Annie Jones had on two occasions visited his camp, he swore that she had not lodged in his tent. General Kilpatrick remained silent on the subject.

The charges were dismissed by the army. However, the gossip surrounding the "confession of Annie Jones" continued throughout their military careers.

One of the most distinctive features of Major General Ambrose E. Burnside was his muttonchop whiskers.

This style of beard became so well known during the Civil War that it found a place in history, and to this day is called burnsides or sideburns.

Major General Joseph "Fighting Joe" Wheeler had the distinction of being the only Confederate officer to gain this same rank in the United States Army.

He fought in the Spanish-American War as a commissioned major general, commanding a corps of volunteers.

Riding long and hard with Wheeler's Confederate Cavalry created a strong thirst in Major John S. Pemberton. After the Civil War, this graduate pharmacist opened a drugstore in Atlanta and experimented with a formula for a new soft drink. Today it is the world's most popular soda, known the world over by its trade name, Coca-Cola.

James Butler Hickok served as a captain of Federal scouts and was also a Union spy for the Western Department of Operations during the Civil War.

As a gunfighter of the Old West, he is remembered by his nickname, "Wild Bill" Hickok.

Quantrill's Raiders were a Southern band of irregular troops responsible for the burning and looting of Lawrence, Kansas, in 1863.

The band consisted of four hundred and fifty men who had no misgivings about attacking Southern sympathizers as well as enemy Union troops. Looked upon with disfavor by Northern and Southern leaders alike, the Raiders, captained by a commissioned Confederate officer, furnished the pioneer West with three of its most infamous outlaws, Jesse and Frank James and Cole Younger.

The famous Italian patriot and freedom fighter Giuseppe Garibaldi was offered a commission in the Army of the United States during the Civil War because of his vast military experience. He was living in this country at the time. He refused.

Wesley Culp, a Confederate private, would have remained an unknown war casualty had it not been for the strange coincidence concerning his birth and death.

He was born and lived on Culp's Hill, near the town of Gettysburg, on property that had been his family's for some time. He died in the Battle of Gettysburg, on the very same piece of property on which he was born.

The "lady spy of the Cumberland" proved not to be a lady. Pauline Cushman, a struggling young actress, took advantage of her natural beauty and charm to help save the Union and achieve for herself a small footnote in the history of this nation.

Her story begins just before the outbreak of the Civil War when at the age of eighteen she was playing small parts in a theatrical variety show in New Orleans. She decided to trade her unsuccessful acting career for marriage and did so by marrying a fellow actor.

The first of many tragedies occurred when four of her children died of diphtheria in one day. Then her husband, who had enlisted in the Union army, died of dysentery. With her family gone, she resumed her stage career, and it is at this point that her exploits as a Union spy had their strange beginnings.

Playing the lead in a show that was to open in Louisville, Kentucky, she was required in one scene to take the center of the stage, raise a glass of champagne and propose a toast. On the night of the opening, the Louisville audience was filled with Southern and Northern sympathizers. When the time came to step forward and make her toast, she did the unexpected and deliberately changed the dialogue. Softly she spoke these lines: "Here's to Jeff Davis and the Southern Confederacy. May the South always maintain her honor and her rights!"

A dead silence fell over the mixed audience. Then, suddenly, there were cheers and catcalls, applause and angry shouts of "Treason!" The Unionists walked out, and the play continued amid an elated and cheering Southern audience.

Pauline Cushman was accepted as a Southern sympathizer. She mingled with Confederate officers and was introduced into a society of loyal Southern partisans. Actually, this was all part of a clever scheme dreamed up by the Louisville Union provost marshal to plant the seed for Pauline's new career as a female Union spy. The plan worked well. The seed germinated, took root, and before long, Pauline was evacuated South along with a group of rebel sympathizers. Once behind Southern lines she visited military installations and charmed Confederate officers into speaking freely about their commands. A flow of invaluable military information was secretly dispatched to Union headquarters.

Eventually, she was exposed as a Union spy. She was searched and found to have maps and drawings of military fortifications secreted in the soles of her shoes. A trial was held and she was sentenced to be hanged, but illness caused her execution to be postponed. Fortunately, Federal armies invaded her Confederate prison and she was set free.

She became a national heroine. President Lincoln commended her for her deeds and she was given the honorary rank of major in the United States Cavalry. Appearing on stage in her major's uniform, she began a series of lectures telling of her adventures as the "lady spy of the Cumberland."

After the war she toured the West, her beauty beginning to fade. Her career as a prostitute began and she was known to have associated with outlaws and gunslingers. A story is told of a day in Tombstone when two rival lovers fought a gun duel over her affections. She personally dressed the loser in preparation for his funeral.

She became addicted to morphine, and in her last years she scrubbed the floors of the very theatre in San Francisco where she had once been acclaimed as an actress and patriot.

At the age of sixty she was found dead in a dingy lodging house in San Francisco. No friends or relatives claimed the body. The GAR (Grand Army of the Republic), the country's leading Civil War veterans' organization, had it moved from the public morgue to a funeral parlor. In the end she received a full military funeral befitting her rank of major in the United States Army.

In the quiet New England town of Terryville, Connecticut, there stands a monument dedicated to one of its courageous sons, Private Dorence Atwater. Halfway around the world is another monument to this Civil War soldier—it rises majestically above his grave on the island of Tahiti.

Atwater was captured in 1864 and confined to the infamous Andersonville Prison in Georgia. There he was assigned work as a clerk in the office of the prison surgeon. His daily routine involved keeping accurate records of the deaths of his fellow prisoners of war.

All that marked the site of a grave in Andersonville was a crude wooden post with a painted number. Atwater carefully registered this number in a roll book along with all other essential details concerning the soldier—his name, date and cause of death, army unit, etc. The roll book was known as the Death Register, and Atwater painstakingly recorded the names of over twelve thousand Union dead.

It was understood that when the war was over the list would be made available to the Federal government as a means of identifying the graves. However, Atwater, knowing the horrible conditions that existed at Andersonville, feared that the original copy of the Death Register would never be turned over, so he secretly made a copy of the list, which he carefully hid in the lining of his coat.

Released from prison a month before the war ended, he set about having his copy published for the benefit of those next of kin who were concerned about their missing relatives. The United States government had meanwhile gained possession of an "official" list, which was somehow missing over twenty-four hundred names.

The government then forced Atwater to turn over his complete copy, threatening him with a court-martial if he did not obey its order. Having no alternative, he gave the list up but did obtain a promise that as soon as the missing twenty-four hundred names were added to the government's list the copy would be returned to him. As compensation, the army bureaucrats paid him $300.

But Atwater's only concern was to see that the list was published to ease the anxiety of those relatives who were eagerly awaiting news of their loved ones. The government's delay in officially publishing moved him to act. After repeated requests for the return of his list were flatly refused, he turned to Clara Barton, founder of the American Red Cross, for help. Her influence broke the government's red tape, and officials were sent to Andersonville for the purpose of correctly marking and identifying the graves of the Union dead. Barton and Atwater were included in the official party. Atwater was furnished with the original Death Register along with his copy.

When the work of lettering and identifying the headboards over the twelve thousand graves was completed, he was requested to return his copy to the authorities. This he steadfastly refused to do, as he still intended to have the list published. For this, he was charged with both conduct to the prejudice of good order and military discipline, and larceny for stealing government property. He was court-martialed, found guilty, sentenced to a dishonorable discharge, fined $300 and sent to prison for eighteen months at hard labor.

Once again Clara Barton rallied to his defense, and, along with other prominent friends, obtained his release from prison after he had served two months of his eighteen-month sentence.

Still determined to have the Death Register published, Atwater consulted Horace Greeley, the famous newspaper editor. With Greeley's help, and in defiance of the government, the book was published and sold for twenty-five cents a copy. This price just covered the printing costs, and no profits were made from its sale. The twelve thousand names it contained proved to be a vital source of information for those relatives still searching for their loved ones.

A great injustice needed to be remedied, because Atwater's court-martial sentence still remained a matter of record. President Andrew Johnson granted Atwater a full pardon and, as a reward, offered him a post as a United States counsul on one of the islands in the South Pacific. In 1871, President Grant had Atwater transferred to the island of Tahiti.

The island natives soon learned to love and respect this stranger from another part of the world. Atwater studied and became proficient in their language, customs and legends. He was adopted by the native royalty of the island and given the Tahitian name of Tupuatooroa, meaning "the wise one." He married a beautiful Tahitian princess and was worshiped as a king by the island natives.

With their help, he established a pearl-diving industry and prospered beyond his wildest dreams. He soon became recognized throughout the Pacific Islands as "the Pearl King of Tahiti." Robert Louis Stevenson, the author, visited him, fascinated by his adventurous life. He later wrote about him in his book *Ebb Tide*. A strong bond of friendship grew between the two men. They entered into business and started the first steamship line between Tahiti and San Francisco. In 1910 Atwater visited San Francisco, and it was during this visit that he became ill and died.

His body was shipped back to his beloved island paradise for burial. At dockside in the small Tahitian harbor, royal native pall-bearers greeted the steamer carrying his body. Thousands of tribal mourners wailed ancient burial chants as royal princes bore his remains on their shoulders to a final resting place over twenty miles away. Noble priests from the king's personal court performed the ritual burial rites, and a granite monument was erected over the grave site.

No Federal officer was more despised by the South than the military commander of New Orleans, Brigadier General Benjamin F. Butler. He was a "political general" with no formal training as a soldier. His authority as commander of the city was one of the blackest periods in Civil War history. Accounts of his ruthlessness toward Southern residents earned him the name of "Beast Butler" and "Butcher Butler," and prompted Jefferson Davis to issue an order that if captured he was to be executed immediately by hanging.

Among his many alleged crimes was his desire to collect silverware without reimbursing the owners. For these acts the local residents named him "Spoons Butler."

He hanged a Southerner for a minor offense, ordered men to take the oath of allegiance to the United States or pay heavy fines, harassed plantation owners by using their slaves for work of his own. But he and his troops were defied by the proud Southern women of New Orleans, who showed their dislike for the Federal occupation forces at every opportunity. They crowded the walks when meeting Union soldiers and made them move aside. From balconies they turned and showed their backsides to approaching Northerners. They emptied slop jars over soldiers' uniforms. When they were shown attention by Union officers, they spat in their faces.

Butler was so enraged at the women's hostile acts that he issued one of the most infamous orders of the war: "When any female shall by word, gesture or movement insult or show contempt for any officer or soldier of the United States, she shall be regarded and held liable to be treated as a woman of the town plying her vocation."

———

For two days during the Battle of Gettysburg, Union brigadier general Alexander Schimmel Pfennig occupied the most embarrassing field position ever held by a commander. After being separated from his troops, General Schimmel Pfennig, in order to avoid capture by rebel forces, took refuge and spent July 2-3, 1863, hiding out in a local pigpen.

———

George Henry Thomas, a major general in the Union army, achieved his greatest victory during the Battle of Nashville in 1864, while officially being relieved of command.

A slow and deliberate tactician, he was criticized for delaying an attack on General Hood's Confederate forces. General Grant issued orders relieving Thomas of command, but before they could be delivered, Thomas began to make his move. In a brilliantly planned battle, he routed the Army of Tennessee and won a magnificent Union victory. He never saw the orders relieving him of command, and they were subsequently withdrawn.

———

This country's highest decoration, the Congressional Medal of Honor, was originated by Congress and approved by President Lincoln in 1861. Initially, the award was authorized for enlisted navy men only. In 1862, the medal was approved for army enlisted men, and in 1863, for army officers. It was not until just before World War I that naval officers were officially permitted to receive it.

———

The Civil War produced three superheroes who were awarded the Congressional Medal of Honor twice. Two were navy men and one served in the army. Both navy men won their awards in coincident but independent actions. Their first medals were presented to them for standing by their guns while under heavy enemy fire, their second for risking their lives while saving fellow seamen.

Lieutenant Thomas W. Custer was the army man who won the medal twice, each time for capturing a Confederate flag. The brother of George Armstrong Custer, he died alongside him at the Battle of the Little Big Horn in 1876.

There is only one case in which the Medal of Honor has been awarded to both father and son.

Arthur MacArthur won his medal in 1863 for gallantry in action during the Civil War Battle of Missionary Ridge. Eighty years later Douglas MacArthur won his medal for his brave defense of a small South Pacific island called Bataan.

There is also only one occasion when two brothers have received the award: The Thompson boys, privates in the Civil War, received citations for bravery after the Battle of Five Forks in 1865.

Approximately ten to fifteen thousand full-blooded American Indians participated in the Civil War. Many of them were recruited from the Five Nation Indian Tribes—Creeks, Chickasaws, Cherokees, Choctaws and Seminoles.

Federal army records show that four thousand Indians served with the Union forces. Of these approximately one-third died.

As the tribes were never happy with government policy, a great many of them joined the Confederate cause. Before the war many had been settled in the South, only to be driven out by Federal troops. Promises by Southern agents of better treaties, more land and greater annuities encouraged Indians to fight against the North.

Strange as it may seem, a good many Southern-bred Indians were slave owners. Seeing Negro slaves alongside teepees tending to the wants of Indian masters raised the eyebrows of many a Federal agent.

In the war some Indian soldiers adopted their traditional style of battle, fighting with tomahawks, bows and arrows and long knives. This led to accusations by both North and South of savage atrocities. At least one Federal soldier was scalped after a battle, and reports of mass scalpings persisted throughout the war.

At army encampments on the eve of a pending battle, regiments of Indian soldiers performed tribal rites, complete with war paint and medicine men warding off evil spirits.

———

Ely Samuel Parker attained the rank of brigadier general while on the personal staff of General Grant. He was instrumental in saving Grant's life during the Battle of Spotsylvania. Present at Appomattox when Lee and Grant met to discuss terms of surrender, he wrote the notes that formed the basis of the final document of surrender.

Despite this man's achievements, he was denied his right to United States citizenship because he was an Indian. His real name was Donehogawa and, a member of the Seneca tribe, he was a fullblooded Indian born on a reservation.

The government at that time did not recognize Indians as citizens of the United States. So Parker, accomplished lawyer and engineer, the highest-ranking Indian in the Union army, was never an American citizen.

———

The long-lasting friendships made between cadets at the United States Military Academy during the pre-Civil War years in part overshadowed the country's sectional and social differences. Accounts of momentary pauses in the business of killing in order to renew old college friendships are recorded in many a soldier's diary.

One such incident took place during the Petersburg campaign.

General Grant heard that Confederate general Pickett had just become a father, and he sent a message across the lines of battle congratulating his old West Point classmate on the happy event. The message was acknowledged, and a few moments later the cannon once again roared over the trenches.

The memoirs and diaries of many Civil War soldiers tell of chance meetings during battle with relatives fighting on the opposite side.

Captain Percival Drayton, a Union naval commander, fired his cannons into a Confederate fortress which he knew was under the command of his brother, assisted by his nephews and a cousin. After the capitulation of the fort, Captain Drayton said, "To think of my pitching here right into such a nest of my relations, my brother, nephews and cousin and others. It is very hard but I cannot exactly see the difference between their fighting against me and I against them except that their cause is as unholy a one as the world has ever seen and mine just the reverse."

It was to this same Captain Drayton that Admiral David Farragut gave the order, "Damn the torpedoes. Full speed ahead!"

Captain Franklin Buchanan, commander of the *Merrimack*, gave orders the morning before the battle with the *Monitor* to set fire to the Federal ship USS *Congress*, at anchor in Hampton Roads, Virginia. On board the *Congress* was his brother, McKean Buchanan.

Clifton K. Prentiss, a captain in the Union army, was among the men who attacked a Confederate fort in Petersburg, Virginia. In the forces opposing them was his brother, Private William S. Prentiss. When the smoke of battle cleared, two soldiers lay wounded side by side, one dressed in blue, the other in gray. Clifton had been struck by a bullet which lodged near his heart, while William had a serious wound in his leg. As they lay suffering together, their eyes met and they clasped hands as brother recognized brother. Their wounds proved fatal on April 2, 1865, just seven days before the war ended.

Forty Confederate generals were born in the North; fifty-two Union generals on Southern soil.

———————

A rather unusual problem confronted the notable Northern general George H. Thomas, who achieved his fame and name as "The Rock of Chickamauga." He was born in Virginia on an archetypal tidewater plantation, and he took some of his slaves to the battle-front to act as his personal servants. Throughout the war he believed in the institution of slavery but fought for the North to help save the Union.

In 1861, when news reached his family in Virginia that he had decided to side with the North, his portrait was turned toward the wall. His sisters, true Southern belles, wrote him a letter requesting that he change his name so as not to bring shame on a loyal and respected Southern family.

The wound that split his family never healed. When Thomas died in 1870, he was given a hero's funeral in the North; but his sisters were conspicuously absent. Questioned regarding their failure to attend, they replied, "Sir, to us our brother died in 1861."

———————

Two opposing officers met under a flag of truce to discuss terms of surrender. After a hard-fought battle the Confederate company under the command of Captain Inglis had captured Union gun positions.

No doubt this battlefield discussion involved some family matters: The Union officer was surrendering to his own brother.

———————

The drama, emotion and sorrow of family separations brought about by the Civil War can best be attested to by the inscription on a monument erected by a grieving father over the common grave of his two soldier sons, one of whom fought for the North and the other for the South: "God Alone Knows Which One Was Right."

After their epic engagement on March 9, 1862, off Hampton Roads, Virginia, the *Monitor* and the *Merrimack*, the ironclad ships that had fought to a draw, met with unfortunate disasters.

The *Merrimack*, in order to avoid capture by Union troops, was scuttled and blown up by her own crew on May 11, 1862, only two months after her historic battle. Seven months later, the *Monitor* sank in rough seas off Cape Hatteras while being towed for repairs. The former crew of the *Merrimack*, now land-based, had failed in its second chance to destroy her. Having joined some Confederate shore batteries, they manned cannons in an attempt to blow her out of the James River. She managed to escape.

No writer could accurately convey the drama behind events that unfolded in the sleepy Southern town of Big Shanty, Georgia, on a hot Saturday afternoon in April 1862. The daring of Union spy James Andrews and the dogged determination of a dynamic Confederate trio, William Fuller, Anthony Murphy and Jeff Cain, set the stage for this incredible war story.

Andrews, a civilian, and twenty-two volunteers, twenty-one of whom were from the army, disguised themselves and boarded the Confederate train the *General*, at Marietta, Georgia. The train proceeded to a small station called Big Shanty. At this point, Andrews and his raiders promptly stole the train, tender and three boxcars right from under the noses of the Confederate soldiers and train personnel. Their aim was to destroy bridges and tracks and otherwise disrupt communication and transportation along this entire Confederate line. As the train pulled out of the station, it was immediately followed down the track by the train conductor, Fuller, along with Anthony Murphy, the station superintendent, and Cain, the engineer. Waving and shouting, this trio attempted to chase the train on foot until they came upon a railroad handcar which they promptly put into use in their pursuit. The handcar had to be abandoned when they came upon a stretch of track the raiders had ripped up in order to prevent their being followed.

Undaunted, they continued the chase on foot until they came upon a small train called the *Yonah*, which they commandeered. The *Yonah* too had to be abandoned when they reached another stretch of ripped-up track.

But they were not to be outdone; once again they continued on foot until they came upon another train, the *William R. Smith*. Taking it over, they continued their pursuit of the *General*.

A few miles up the track, they met another train, called the *Texas*, which, however, was pointed in the wrong direction. They boarded it and continued the chase, with the *Texas* running backward.

Even so, the train gained on the *General*, and the raiders could see that it was about to overtake them. In an effort to halt it, they set fire to one of the boxcars. However, it began to rain and the car would not catch fire.

The raiders next attempted to uncouple the boxcars, hoping to ram the oncoming train. But the engineer of the *Texas*, seeing the uncoupled cars, reversed his engine, coupled the cars onto his train, and went on again with the chase.

Running out of fuel and not being able to outdistance the *Texas*, the raiders abandoned the *General* and attempted to make their way back to Union lines. In a week they were all captured, and Andrews and seven of his companions were hanged. Some time later all but six of those remaining escaped. The six were afterward paroled and returned to duty. The entire group of raiders, including those who were hanged, were awarded the first Congressional Medals of Honor to be issued by the United States.

An interesting fact to note is that during the entire chase the raiders outnumbered their pursuers. If they had known this, they might have stood their ground and completed their mission.

One of the most daring cavalry raids of the Civil War, Grierson's Raid, was led by Benjamin Henry Grierson. He took his seventeen hundred Union troops through the very heart of the Confederacy, destroying transportation facilities and arousing fear in Tennessee, Mississippi and Louisiana.

Even more extraordinary is the still-unproven claim that Grierson disliked horses.

———

By far the number-one capital military crime in the Federal army was desertion. Over two hundred thousand soldiers deserted and less than seventy-five thousand were ever caught.

Official military records show that 267 Union soldiers were tried and executed for military crimes. Of this number, 72 were executed for murder, 23 for rape, 20 for mutiny, 3 for spying, 4 for theft, 4 for other offenses and 141 for military desertion. No records exist of military executions among Confederate forces.

———

It was a grim day on August 19, 1863: Twenty-five thousand people were assembled at Rappahannock Station to witness the execution of five Union soldiers convicted of desertion. As the 118th Pennsylvania Regimental Band played the traditional "Death March," the condemned soldiers marched slowly behind their coffins. The coffins were then placed beside freshly dug graves, and each of the five soldiers stood at attention, hands manacled behind their backs, eyes blindfolded.

The command to fire was given and thirty-six bullets exploded into the air. The five soldiers toppled backward. Their bodies were placed in the coffins, and three clergymen stepped forward to perform the burial service. Standing side by side, they ministered the final burial prayers. There were a Protestant minister for the three Protestant soldiers, a Catholic priest for the Catholic soldier and a rabbi for the Jewish soldier.

This marked the first recorded case in American history of an all-denominational military funeral service.

———

So acute was the shortage of able-bodied soldiers in the Confederate army that by 1864 there were over ten thousand amputees listed on the muster rolls as present for duty.

During the Vietnam War, a number of unwilling draftees escaped to Canada to avoid service in the army. This was also a pattern in 1863, as revealed in a brief quotation from the book *Hardtack and Coffee*, by John D. Billings, a soldier in the Civil War.

Referring to several Civil War draftees, he wrote, "Yet another had suddenly gone to Canada on important business—which was a favorite refuge for all those who were afraid of being forced into service."

The Union army had soldier shirkers and slackers who made a career of avoiding anything connected with "work" details. But when the day of battle arrived, these loud-mouthed heroes would suddenly be discovered on, for example, stretcher-bearer teams which carried the wounded to the rear. Their fellow soldiers referred to these "goldbrickers" of the 1860s as "beats."

A senator from Georgia described Confederate "beats" as "invincible in peace and invisible in war."

Some of the more illiterate Civil War recruits did not know their left feet from their right, and this posed a problem for drill sergeants. They overcame this by tying small bits of straw to a recruit's right foot and bits of hay to his left. Then they drilled the recruit by barking out orders of "hay foot," "straw foot," "hay foot," "straw foot."

Throughout the war, the green recruit was known as a "straw foot."

The term doughboy, used to describe the American soldier,

dates back to the Civil War when Union infantrymen wore buttons on their uniforms that resembled balls of dough.

"GI" was also used during the war; at the time, it meant galvanized iron.

The familiar military shoulder patch worn by today's American soldier in order to designate his branch of military service was the inspiration of Major General Philip Kearny, a Civil War officer who died in battle in 1862.

The kind of general who led his men into battle, he desired to create pride and an esprit de corps among the soldiers of his command. So he issued an order that a round piece of red cloth be worn on their caps to identify them as soldiers in his brigade. It became known as the Kearny Patch.

Before long, other units adopted their own color patches, and on March 21, 1863, the headquarters of the Army of the Potomac, under Major General Hooker, made the idea official. All army corps were ordered to wear badges of differing colors and designs symbolizing their individual units.

The army bugle call known as "Taps" was composed by a Civil War Union commander, General Daniel Butterfield, in July 1862.

Pup tents were the most commonly used shelters issued to soldiers during the Civil War. They were referred to, however, as dog tents.

The principal mode of transportation used by the Union and Southern armies throughout the Civil War was the army horse. It was estimated that the Union army alone used over six hundred fifty thousand horses for all types of conveyances.

To distinguish unbroken mules and horses from the rest of the herd, the army developed the practice of shaving the tails of these animals. In time the word shavetails was used to refer not only to these untrained animals but also to newly recruited lieutenants.

In the 1860s, sutlers were the equivalent of our Army PXs. They were civilians who traveled with their wagonloads of merchandise right behind the troops, and were authorized by military commanders to sell their homemade wares to soldiers.

Most of the time their merchandise was of low quality; yet they charged high prices, making themselves the most unpopular civilians in camp.

One of their most popular products was whiskey. Its quality was so poor that soldiers coined the term red eye for the whiskey because of the unsightly red eyes that came with the hangover it produced. The words rot gut referred to the irritating effects the whiskey had on a soldier's stomach.

The two most common vices of Civil War soldiers were drinking and gambling.

During the Battle of Bull Run, rebel troops captured a complete "faro bank" card game found in the tent of some enterprising Yankee soldier. Gambling was illegal, but as the din of battle subsided, the rebels saw to it that the first tent staked was the faro bank gambling casino. They invited all to try their luck and much attention was soon focused on the tent.

Word reached the colonel of the regiment, A. P. Hill, who at once had it raided. To the colonel's embarrassment, the raid produced some unforeseen results. Along with the many enlisted soldiers in the tent were several prominent officers of the regiment and a distinguished Confederate politician who was visiting his soldier son.

In 1861, the United States Capitol housed an army bakery that produced sixteen thousand loaves of fresh bread daily for Union forces.

———

Suffering the loneliness of being away from home and family, the Civil War soldier frequently would carry on a "lonely hearts" correspondence with some young woman who was sensitive to the lack of male companionship caused by the war. She would advertise for a soldier "pen pal" in one of the several popular magazines or newspapers of the 1860s.

In the *Waverly Magazine,* one such advertisement requested a "soldier correspondent, who must not be over twenty, who desires to write to a young woman of eighteen, of prepossessing appearance, good education and would exchange photographs, if desired, for the purpose of mutual companionship."

———

Pinups, a favorite diversion of the lonely modern soldier, played no less a part in barracks life in the 1860s. Of course, there were no "centerfold" beauties to adorn army tents, but soldiers were willing customers for the pictorial erotica documented in the following 1864 mail order circular:

NEW PICTURES FOR BACHELORS

The following series of pictures, size 12 x 15, are all highly colored and fit for framing. We send them by mail, post paid, for 12 cents each. $1.20 cents per dozen, all one kind or assorted as desired.

"*The Wood-Nymphs' Frolic.*" The group of Girls which this picture represents, are engaged in a rustic dance, while one of the party plays a tambourine. These beautiful beings sport in all the consciousness of innocence, caring little whether or not they are seen in their nude and interesting frolic. Price 12 cents.

"*A Bed-room Bombardment.*" This picture represents half a dozen young boarding-school Misses, engaged in a "lark" before they had time to dress themselves. Some of their pranks are so funny as to really make the maidens blush, but they are too earnestly engaged in their sport, and don't see it. It is truly a rare and spirited picture of female charms. Price 12 cents.

"*Toilet Mysteries.*" A picture for a bachelor's bedroom for which the girls would pull any body's hair if they were allowed to look in upon it. It represents some half a dozen beautiful young girls dressing themselves for a fancy ball. Price 12 cents.

"*Storming the Enemy's Breastworks.*" This is decidedly one of the best pictures we have ever seen of the kind. It represents an amorous Union soldier while playing with a Secesh maiden, making a very indelicate assault, the girl don't seem exactly to like, nor does she say emphatically no. Under the circumstances we must conclude that the Breastworks unconditionally surrendered. Send for the picture and contemplate the scene. Price 12 cents.

"*Girls Bathing a Scene in the Woods.*" A party of beautiful young girls on a hot summer's day, desiring to enjoy the luxury of a cool spring water bath, have taken the liberty to do so in the woods. Price 12 cents.

"*The Temptation of St. Anthony.*" This is a beautiful illustration of how Satan, when failing in all other ways to tempt St. Anthony, transformed his familiars into beautiful girls. Those bewitching creatures overwhelm the pious hermit with their caresses when he involuntary raises his eyes, leers at their naked charms and all is lost. This is a spirited and spicy scene. Price 12 cents.

The Civil War soldier frequently used the mail to send money home to his dependent family. On many occasions, it never reached the intended destination, and as a result, authorities introduced the postal money order service in 1864.

Civil War pension legislation was approved unanimously by the United States Congress on July 14, 1862. It applied only to Union soldiers or their widows. Southern states awarded their own pensions to Confederate veterans.

It was not until 1958 that Congress passed special legislation authorizing pensions for the widows of Confederate veterans. They were also awarded to the last two surviving Confederate soldiers.

How ironic that these two men were granted pensions from a government that one hundred years before they had fought to destroy.

Memorial Day, the holiday that honors our country's dead soldiers, was suggested to Congress in 1868 by a veterans' association, the Grand Army of the Republic. Its original purpose was to set aside a day to remember those who died during the Civil War.

During the early twentieth century, there existed an unofficial code among the sculptors of Civil War monuments. The code they agreed upon was this: If an officer served throughout the war without having been wounded, then he would be seated upon a horse whose four feet were grounded; if the officer was wounded, the horse would have one foot raised; if the officer was killed in action, both the horse's front feet would be off the ground.

Kensington, Connecticut, made the pages of history by erecting the first monument to honor the Civil War dead. Constructed in July 1863, two years before the end of the war, it cost $350.

The last surviving soldier of the Civil War died in 1959, marking the passing of the "old sarges" who told their wild yarns of battlefield heroics to the children of our century.

Yet links to that great past remain. On January 9, 1972, the author taped an interview in Winsted, Connecticut, with Mrs. Maude Ball, age eighty-seven, who was married to a private in Company B of the First Connecticut Artillery. She related her fascinating story with great pride and dignity.

In 1861, her husband, Charles Ball, enlisted in the Union army; he was thirteen at the time, but lied about his age. They married in 1911, when she was twenty-six years old, and he used to tell her of his meeting President Lincoln and General Grant. Every year on Memorial Day, the town of Winsted provided a special car for her to ride in during the parade.

Shortly after our interview, Mrs. Ball passed away. She had been receiving a veteran's pension of $125 per month.

V

"Beans Killed More Than Bullets"

The Civil War killed more Americans than any other war. Six hundred thousand men from both North and South died in just four years. Only one-third of this number were killed in actual battle; disease accounted for the other deaths.

Six million cases of illness were reported during the war. Diarrhea and dysentery incapacitated more soldiers than any other disease. In the first year of the war, the reported sick rate from these two diseases was 640 per 1,000 men. In the second year of the war, the sick rate rose to 995 per 1,000 men. The final statistics showed that diarrhea and dysentery took the lives of 44,558 soldiers.

"Beans killed more than bullets" was an expression used by military surgeons after an outbreak of diarrhea was caused by some bean soup.

The source of "death from the frying pan," another popular comment of the time, was the soldier's habit of cooking all his rations in whatever fat or grease he may have had on hand in order to make his food more palatable. Infections resulted and remained unchecked because of the poor hygiene in the camps.

In 1861, the medical corps consisted of only 98 officers; there were 11,000 by the end of the war.

97

The medical corps was so poorly organized at first that during the months of October, November and December 1861, 2,881 men were discharged for disabilities they had had at the time of their enlistment.

The rout of Federal troops at the Battle of Bull Run was so complete that not a single wounded Federal soldier reached Washington in an ambulance. Civilian ambulance drivers left the field at the early stages of the battle, and fleeing Federal soldiers commandeered the vehicles to speed their retreat to Washington.

Wounded soldiers who feared capture performed some remarkable acts of endurance under the influence of panic. A soldier who had just had his arm amputated on the battlefield walked the twenty-seven miles back to Washington. Another walked the distance with a large hole through both thighs and the scrotum. A third walked there with holes in both cheeks, a broken jaw and a nearly torn-off tongue. Still another reached Washington despite bullet holes through both calves.

Infection from wounds was one of the primary causes of death during the Civil War.

Thousands of victims might have been saved had Sir Joseph Lister developed antiseptic surgery in 1861 rather than in 1865.

Civil War surgeons honed their scalpels on the soles of their shoes as they operated with pus-covered instruments.

Fundamental techniques used by surgeons then involved three basic elements. For local irritation and infection, a Spanish fly blister was administered. If this failed, scalding water and flaming alcohol paper were applied to the wound.

For relief of pain, moxa was applied. This consisted of a wad of cotton heated and burned onto the skin over the painful area. For pneumonia, a variation of "bleeding," known as cupping, was used. A small amount of alcohol was ignited in a cup and applied to the chest until a blister appeared. The blister was lanced and a small amount of blood extracted. This was done over and over again, the patient suffering from pain, his body inflicted with a mass of scars.

General Carl Schurz offered this description of a typical Civil War operation:

Most of the operating tables were placed in the open where the light was best, some of them partially protected against the rain by tarpaulins or blankets stretched upon poles. There stood the surgeons, their sleeves rolled up to their elbows, their bare arms as well as their linen aprons smeared with blood, their knives not seldom held between their teeth, while they were helping a patient on or off the table or had their hands otherwise occupied. ... As a wounded man was lifted on the table, often shrieking with pain as the attendants handled him, the surgeon quickly examined the wound and resolved upon cutting off the injured limb. Some ether was administered and the body put in position in a moment. The surgeon snatched his knife from between his teeth ... wiped it rapidly once or twice across his bloodstained apron, and the cutting began. The operation accomplished, the surgeon would look around with a deep sigh, and then ... "Next!"

And from a surgeon comes this vivid story of contamination:

We operated in old blood-stained and often pus-stained coats, the veterans of a hundred fights. We operated with clean hands in the social sense, but they were undisinfected hands. We used undisinfected instruments from undisinfected plush-lined cases and, still worse, used marine sponges which had been used in prior pus cases and had been only washed in tap water. If a sponge or an instrument fell on the floor, it was washed and squeezed in a basin of tap water and used as if it were clean.

Speed with the scalpel was the mark of a top army surgeon. One doctor wrote in his medical report that it took him but two and a half minutes to amputate a limb and sixteen minutes to remove a breast "with armpit dissection." Rarely did a Civil War surgical operation last an hour or more.

It is interesting to note that Civil War surgeons' reports showed that the mortality rate for amputations was higher when the amputation was closer to the trunk of the body. Amputation of the toe or finger had a 2 percent mortality rate, amputation at the ankle a 13 percent rate, amputation of the lower leg 26 percent, amputation at the hip joint 85 percent. Removal of the lower arm resulted in a 20 percent mortality rate, of the entire arm a 40 percent mortality rate.

Convalescence after major surgery usually lasted a year or more and was accompanied by a long hospital stay. Minor surgery required a six-week convalescence.

Because of the many amputations performed by Civil War surgeons, the term sawbones was coined to describe them.

In 1861, there were only twenty clinical thermometers in the entire Union army, although they had been commonly used in medical practice for hundreds of years.

The Army Medical Department did not have a single achromatic microscope until 1863.

The stethoscope, considered a novelty, was not widely used during the war.

Nor was the hypodermic syringe in common use. The majority of Civil War doctors preferred to "dust" morphine into open wounds or prescribe pills of opium.

Only a handful of Civil War physicians knew how to operate the ophthalmoscope, a device for eye examinations invented in 1851.

Among the many medical advances made at the time of the Civil War was the technique developed by Confederate surgeons for collapsing a lung that had been damaged beyond repair by a Union bullet.

The Civil War was the first American war during which medical histories were kept and pathological specimens collected for analysis.

Bullets were responsible for 94 percent of Civil War wounds. The one most commonly used was a .58-caliber conoidal lead projectile called the Minié ball. Because of its size and low velocity, it lost its shape upon penetration and left a large wound which almost always became infected. Often it also shattered the bone. Today's bullet leaves a clean hole and, because of its high velocity, usually passes completely through the body. Its speed in penetrating generates heat, which often has the effect of sterilizing the wound and causing less bleeding.

The chances of surviving a battle wound during the Civil War were only one in seven, whereas in the Korean conflict of the 1950s, of every fifty men wounded only one died.

The disease responsible for the most deaths during the Civil War was typhoid. The most common ailment was diarrhea, which the soldiers called "the Tennessee quick-step." Some soldiers used to say, "Bowels are of more consequence than brains in the army."

Venereal disease, as in every war, took its toll among the troops. Officially, one out of every twelve Union soldiers contracted the disease. It was so rampant among Confederate troops that Southern hospitals instituted special venereal disease wards, and Dr. S. H. Stout, a Southern army surgeon, established a hospital devoted exclusively to its treatment.

The miracle drugs of today were unknown in the 1860s. One accepted method of treating venereal disease involved swallowing pills made of pine resin and blue vitriol and then downing a shot of whiskey.

The Civil War was responsible for the first cases of drug addiction in the United States. Morphine, then a new drug, was indiscriminately used by army doctors to ease the pain of wounded soldiers. Many then became addicts. As the effects of the drug were not yet known, doctors described what we call the process of addiction as "army disease."

Whiskey and brandy were used as universal stimulants by doctors in the Civil War. A sixteen-year-old soldier in a St. Louis hospital was kept alive by the administering of thirty-six ounces of brandy to him every day. Another patient was given forty-eight ounces of eggnog and two or three bottles of port every day for several weeks. Still another received a half pint of egg and brandy every two hours. In an attempt to keep a soldier alive, one doctor prescribed as much of this mixture as the patient could take.

We do not know whether any of these soldiers survived, but if they died, then at least they died happy.

Although the anesthetics ether and chloroform were administered in operations before the Civil War, many surgeons of 1861 thought them too dangerous to be used as part of standard practice.

Nevertheless, chloroform was the main anesthetic used during the war. Approximately eighty thousand general anesthetics were administered during the entire Civil War; 76 percent were of chloroform, 14 percent of ether, and 9 percent were a mixture of the two. Of those receiving anesthetics, 37 percent died from chloroform, 4 percent from ether and 2 percent from their mixture.

One of the most interesting lessons learned from wartime treatment of wounds came about as the result of a lack of antiseptic supplies in the Civil War.

A group of wounded Confederate prisoners was left unattended in a prison stockade, denied the necessary dressings for their open wounds because of the lack of medical supplies. In a short time it was noticed that the wounds, which were exposed to the open air, became infested with maggots. Normal procedure demanded that the wounds be cleansed at once, but the doctors were too busy ministering to the injuries of Union soldiers. Much to the doctors' surprise, the infected wounds healed rapidly, while the bandaged and dressed wounds of the Union soldiers continued to need attention. Investigation proved that the maggots performed a scavenging job, eating only diseased tissue and allowing healthy tissue to cleanse the wound.

To avoid the draft, Civil War recruits devised some ingenious schemes to fool the examining physicians. One of the more frequent frauds involved pretending one had a hernia. It was easy for the doctor to spot a recruit wearing a truss upside down or backward, but the technique of blowing air through small punctures in the scrotum was harder to detect.

Self-inflicted mutilations were in some cases used to escape the draft. Fingers and toes were intentionally cut off, and when it was discovered that the army required good teeth as a prerequisite for induction, there suddenly appeared an uncommon number of draftees without theirs. The army put great emphasis on the quality of teeth because a soldier had to bite off the end of his paper cartridge in order to fire his weapon. Also, the basic food ration known as hardtack was difficult to chew without good molars.

Physicians documented cases of men who tried to create disqualifying symptoms by artificial means. Chronic eye diseases were often due to the presence of sand or cayenne pepper underneath the eyelids. Skin diseases were created by applying hot lye or sulfuric acid to an area of the body. Tightly binding an arm or a leg for several hours would produce simulated varicose veins. Applying croton oil or cayenne pepper to the anus produced hemorrhoids.

A draftee once appeared before an examining doctor with a specimen of his urine which, on analysis, seemed to indicate that the man was dying of Bright's disease. He was requested to provide another specimen in the presence of the doctor, and it was then that he confessed his deception. The urine he had submitted was really that of a dying friend.

Several examining physicians reported being offered bribes. One draftee attempted to bribe an examining doctor with "favors from [his] female friends." Dr. William W. Mayo, father of the brothers who founded the Mayo Clinic, was dismissed from the Federal army because of a scandal involving a bribe.

In contrast to those attempting to escape army service, there were men who did all they could to enlist by disguising their ages or illnesses.

A physician's examination of an underweight recruit revealed the soles of his shoes to be made of lead. Ice packs applied to hernias for a day or two before a physical would cause the hernias to recede.

In order to appear younger, old men would dye their hair, shave their beards and camouflage their false teeth by staining them with tobacco juice. Young boys of thirteen or fourteen would write the number 18 on a piece of paper and place it in the soles of their shoes. They would then appear before the recruiting officer to be sworn in, and in good conscience raise their right hand and swear that they were "over eighteen."

A prominent South Carolina doctor who served with the Confederate medical corps was Dr. Simon Baruch. His son, the famed elder statesman Bernard Baruch, was advisor to Presidents.

In 1861 the United States had only one military hospital, and that had a capacity of forty beds. But after the war started, almost every major city in both North and South built hospitals to house the sick and wounded soldiers. In Richmond alone there were forty-two.

There is no official record of the death rate in all Confederate hospitals, but Chimborazo Hospital, the largest in Richmond, reported a rate of 9 percent. The Federal Army Hospital, Lincoln Hospital in Washington, was reported to have a death rate of over 14 percent.

The above figures do not speak well for these institutions, but when one considers that by the end of the conflict approximately 17,500 Union and Confederate doctors had treated over 3 million soldiers, one appreciates their tremendous undertaking in the face of the limited medical knowledge of the time.

Union hospitals that accepted men from all units of the military rather than from just one branch of service were called military general hospitals. Starting in 1861, they were established by the taking over of buildings previously used for other purposes. In Washington, a jail, a hotel, a girls' school, a church and a warehouse were converted into military general hospitals. In Philadelphia, a railroad station, a coach factory and a silk mill were taken over. In Newark and Elmira, several hospitals had once been furniture factories.

At first, these general hospitals functioned badly because they were ill-equipped. A determined effort to improve them resulted in a hospital system that was one of the wonders of the medical world. By the end of the war, these hospitals had cared for 1,057,052 soldiers with a mortality rate of only 8 percent. At the time, this was the lowest rate ever recorded in military hospitals, including those in Europe.

At the beginning of the war, officers who were wounded were not permitted to enter army hospitals. They were considered salaried men and even had to pay for their own rations. Army hospitals were provided for enlisted men only.

By 1864, however, the War Department had established several officers' hospitals. Patients were charged a dollar a day, plus thirty cents extra if a personal servant boarded with them.

The first organized ambulance system was introduced during the Civil War. Military band musicians laid aside their instruments during battle engagements and acted as ambulance attendants and stretcher-bearers to move the wounded to the rear, thus giving the front-line soldiers no excuse to leave the battle in order to help the wounded. Before the advent of these stretcher-bearers, it was not uncommon to see six, or even eight, soldiers leave the line to carry one wounded man to the dressing station.

By 1864, some divisions of the Army of the Potomac had given up using regimental musicians for ambulance work and hospital details. "Musicians and blood" apparently did not mix. A Medical Department order charged that the musicians "proved utterly worthless in bringing off the wounded, behaving with the utmost cowardice, and required more persons to watch and see that they did their duty than their services were worth." It also stated that they were "adverse to labor or danger, and habitually insubordinate." When a field hospital came under fire, they would usually disappear.

Smuggling desperately needed medical supplies into the South through Federal lines was a hazardous task, and, in many cases, was accomplished by women.

Their many crinoline petticoats, surrounded by wide hoopskirts, and their long bouffant-styled hair capped by broad bonnets made excellent hiding places. No chivalrous Union picket would dare search the person of a pretty Southern belle who, with dimpled smile, could easily pass through Federal lines.

One instance when a pretty smile failed to distract alert Federal guards involved Louisa P. Buckner, who was captured and imprisoned as a Confederate spy. She was caught smuggling valuable quinine in the folds of her skirt. It was later revealed that she was the niece of the Union postmaster general.

———

Dr. Mary Edward Walker was undoubtedly the champion feminist of the 1860s. She graduated from medical school in 1855, the only woman in her class. Because of the prejudice of the day, she was able to practice medicine only under the most trying of circumstances. To ease some of her problems with fellow physicians, she wore men's clothing rather than conventional dresses. Her attire consisted of trousers, a fitted man's dress coat and a man's top hat.

Far ahead of her time, she insisted on having the minister omit from her wedding ceremony the words "honor and obey" and then she steadfastly refused to give up her maiden name. She supported all causes defending women's rights.

When the Civil War began, she presented her medical credentials to the War Department and requested an immediate commission as a surgeon in the Union army. Although the need for experienced doctors was great, officials felt a female surgeon was out of the question. The army refused to accept her professional credentials.

Undeterred, Dr. Walker went, at her own expense, to General Burnside's Virginia headquarters and volunteered her services for field hospital duty. The wounded were coming in by the thousands and her skills could not be ignored. She was immediately accepted. Working side by side with male physicians, she earned their respect and was unofficially permitted to wear a Union officer's uniform with the green sash of an army surgeon.

Eventually she was appointed civilian surgeon with the army, earning eighty dollars a month, and was transferred to the Army of the Cumberland. There, male physicians objected to a woman doctor, and her services were confined to routine orderly duties. Rebelling, she began to tend to the medical needs of civilians in the area, and was captured and imprisoned in a Richmond prisoner-of-war camp. She was exchanged for another prisoner after several months in the camp.

For her meritorious service during the war, Dr. Walker was awarded the Medal of Honor on November 11, 1865, the only woman ever to receive it. Her postwar activity involved fighting for women's rights, most notably women's suffrage. At one point she sent to Congress a suffragist petition with over thirty-five thousand signatures.

Her Medal of Honor pinned to her officer's uniform, she lectured throughout the country, giving an account of her experiences during the war and at the same time speaking out for women's rights. Her lecture tours proved financially unprofitable. In 1887 she began appearing in carnival sideshows along with freaks and circus curiosities. In 1917 Congress retroactively removed her name from the list of Medal of Honor winners because she had not actively risked her life in combat. Fifty years after it had been awarded, she was asked to return her medal to Congress. Bitter and angry, she refused.

Two years later, at the age of eighty-six, she fell while climbing the steps of the Capitol on her way to make one last appeal to Congress to let her keep her medal. She died as a result of this fall, a sad and forgotten woman.

Now there is talk in Congress of restoring her medal to her in recognition of her military service. There is also speculation that the actual reason it was taken from her centered around her involvement with civil libertarian causes.

Captain Sally Tompkins had the unique distinction of being the only woman to hold an official commission in the Army of the Confederate States. She earned her commission by independently establishing a soldiers' hospital in Richmond. Known as the Robertson Hospital, it soon achieved an outstanding reputation for saving the wounded.

With her small staff of volunteer Richmond ladies, this tireless, devoted woman became the envy of the Confederate Medical Department, and it was not long before wounded men requested transfers to her hospital.

Word of Sally Tompkins' accomplishments reached the ears of Jefferson Davis. When the Confederate government officially took over the administration of all military hospitals, Davis immediately commissioned her a captain in the army to enable her to remain the head of her hospital. She accepted the appointment but refused the pay that went with it.

Captain Sally, as she was called, lived some fifty years after the war. In old age, she was penniless, forced to reside in a Confederate women's home. Because she was a member of the Confederate veterans' organization, her death did not pass unnoticed and she was buried with full military honors.

———

Under the guidance of Dr. Elizabeth Blackwell, the first woman physician in the United States, an unofficial female nurse corps was established as early as April 25, 1861, only thirteen days after the Civil War had begun.

———

The Civil War had its Florence Nightingale in Dorothea Dix, who initiated reforms in the nursing profession at a time when women were first gaining acceptance as nurses.

The Civil War introduced women nurses to military hospitals, and Dix's appearance on the scene in 1861 moved one prominent leader to say, "The month of April 1861 was distinguished not more by the universal springing of the grass than by the uprising of the women of the land."

She was appointed superintendent of female nurses in June 1861, and in August, Congress gave female nurses legal status and provided for their wages. The salary was forty cents a day and one full ration.

Dix immediately set up standards for qualifying as a nurse. Candidates had to be past thirty, healthy, "plain almost to repulsion in dress and devoid of personal attractions." They had to have a knowledge of "how to cook all kinds of low diet" and be prepared to renounce "colored dresses, hoops, curls, jewelry, and flowers on their bonnets." Reading, writing and neatness were required. It was expected that they be in their own rooms at "Taps," or nine o'clock, unless they had to tend to patients, and they could not visit any patient or officer except on business. The forty cents a day received from the government had to be used to supplement rations; any money left over was to go toward the welfare of patients.

Approximately thirty-two hundred women served as nurses during the war; the ratio of women nurses to men averaged one to five.

Louisa May Alcott, author of *Little Women*, served as a nurse during the Civil War. Her first book, *Hospital Sketches*, was based on her experiences in the wards.

A widow from Iowa, Mrs. Anne Wittemeyer, introduced the first hospital soft foods diet. It catered to the needs of individual soldier patients and proved to be such a success that before long it was adopted by all Union hospitals as standard dietary routine.

A woman of strength and stubbornness, Mary Bickerdyke was known to her "boys in blue" as "Mother" Bickerdyke. Working unofficially as a nurse, she did not hesitate to fight hospital surgeons and generals in an effort to overcome military bureaucracy and hospital inefficiency.

General Sherman, having received countless complaints from his surgeons regarding "Mother" Bickerdyke's interference, lightheartedly remarked, "She ranks me."

As a symbol of the enduring affection which the common soldier held for this unselfish woman, she was permitted to march in the ranks along with "her boys" in the Grand Army victory parade in Washington at the end of the war.

Both Union private W. H. Brown and Confederate artillery major Richard Snowden Andrews were given up for dead on the battlefield; their survival constitutes a tribute to man's determination to stay alive.

Private Brown engaged in a skirmish against a band of Confederate guerrillas at Cow Creek, Kansas. At the end of the battle, he weighed one pound more than when it had begun; sixteen lead Minié balls weighing a total of one pound three and one-half ounces had penetrated the entire length of his body. Left for dead, he lay on the battlefield for five days without nourishment or attention of any kind. When found alive by a burial party, he was transferred to an area hospital. Surgeons were amazed when he began to recover, particularly since several bullets had passed through his skull. Equally astounding was the fact that this soldier, weakened as he was by his wounds, survived for five days without food or water, exposed to the dangers of shock, hemorrhage, infection, gangrene and tetanus.

Major Andrews was hit by an artillery shell that exploded directly in front of him during the Battle of Cedar Mountain. Shell fragments tore a gaping hole in his abdominal wall. His entire stomach and intestines were exposed. The following on-the-spot medical report is by Dr. Thomas B. Amiss, who attended to his wounds:

With my brother, Dr. William H. Amiss, surgeon of the 60th Georgia Regiment, we arrived at the roadside and found the wounded man a few feet inside of a field. I dismounted and going up to him saw his bowels were out and called back to my brother, "The only thing to do to this man is to dig a hole and put him in it."

The wounded man aroused and replied, "That is what Dr. McGuire told me. If you damned doctors would do something for me, I would get well." I said, "My friend, do you know that your bowels are all out and covered by chickweed, clay dust and sand?" He again replied, "I had a hound dog run a mile with his guts out and catch a fox and I know I am as good as a dog and can stand as much."

I said to my brother, "This man is full of all sorts of grit (meaning sand from the road and physical stamina as well) and we will do what we can for him." I ordered my litter bearers to carry him on the dining room table and proceeded to clean his wound which was caused by a shell from the enemy's gun which tore away the abdominal wall, crushed the bones of the right hip and narrowly missed the intestine.

My brother, Dr. William H. Amiss, washed out the abdominal cavity removing therefrom a handful of sand and vegetable matter. The point of the hip bone was broken and hanging down. This was cut off. The work was all carefully done with salt solution. The sewing up of the wound, about seven inches long, I did with ordinary boss cotton and a calico needle.

Andrews lived a full and distinguished life. British medical men who studied his case concluded that his recovery was due to the foreign material in his peritoneal cavity. Thus the new medical technique of placing dust in the abdominal wounds of soldiers, practiced during the Franco-Prussian War, was developed.

———

One of the Civil War's most curious battle wounds was suffered by Private Edmond Brewer Tate of the Confederate army during the Battle of Chickamauga.

A Yankee bullet tore through his left breast at the nipple, raced downward and came out his back. It was believed that the bullet had penetrated his heart and he was left for dead on the battlefield. As luck would have it, his brothers found his body and discovered he was still alive.

They took him to the army field doctor, who found that his heart was still beating, not on the left side but on the right. After careful examination it was concluded that the force of the bullet had knocked Private Tate's heart to the opposite side.

After the war he lived to a ripe old age and was forever known as "the man whose heart was knocked to the wrong side at Chickamauga."

———

Incredible as this story may seem it was duly recorded and remains a part of the medical history of the Union Army. It took place in Virginia on May 12, 1863, and was reported by acting Army Field Surgeon Captain L. G. Capers.

Capers' regiment was engaged in a skirmish with Confederate troops on the outskirts of a small Virginia village. The firing was spasmodic, with sharpshooters picking off men on both sides. About one hundred yards behind the Union regiment stood a large house. On its steps, a mother and her two young daughters watched the action and prepared to act as nurses if called upon to do so. Suddenly, a young Union soldier was hit and fell almost in front of Captain Capers. At the same moment, a scream was heard coming from the steps.

Capers immediately examined the soldier's wound and found that the bullet had broken his leg and then ricocheted upward and torn through his scrotum. Giving him temporary aid, the doctor was met by the lady of the house, who was in a state of shock. She cried out that one of her daughters had been shot and begged the doctor to come quickly to her aid. The captain, having done all he could for the soldier, examined the daughter and discovered that a bullet had punctured her abdominal wall. He searched for the bullet but could not determine its location, so he made her as comfortable as possible.

Eight months later, Capers' regiment was once again on picket duty in that same area. He paid a courtesy call at the big house and what he found left him astounded: the wounded daughter was in an advanced stage of pregnancy!

The girl repeatedly swore that she had never been intimate with anyone, but four weeks later she gave birth to an eight-pound boy. The baby bore an uncanny likeness to the soldier wounded nine months earlier.

Capers theorized that the bullet that wounded the soldier, having entered and passed through his scrotum, carried sperm cells on it. This same bullet lodged in the girl's uterus, impregnating her.

The story has a happy ending. The soldier, having fully recovered from his wound, successfully courted the daughter and married her. Two more children were born without any help from Confederate sharpshooters.

Dr. F. Donald Napolitani, a New York physician, investigated the case as reported by Captain Capers, and in the *New York State Journal of Medicine* dated February 1, 1959, insists that such a set of circumstances could actually have happened.

In 1862, a Louisiana planter suggested smuggling a blanket infected with yellow fever germs into the city of New Orleans. The idea of creating an epidemic in that Federally held city over one hundred years ago was nothing more than a forerunner of germ warfare.

The Civil War might have had its "Hiroshima" in 1861 had the plan suggested by a young Confederate private been acted upon by Southern officials.

The National Archives in Washington contains a letter written by Private Isham Walker to the Confederate Secretary of War, L. P. Walker. Here is an excerpt from that letter:

> Camp Magnolia Near Pensacola, Florida
> June 4th/61

Hon. L. P. Walker
Secretary of War

... Inclosed please find a rough sketch of my plan for bombarding Pickins and the fleet from a balloon held in equilibrium by 4 copper wires anchored as shown and at an altitude of two miles, drop poisonous bombs into the fortress and fleet. ...

... for the attack upon Pickins I propose to place in the bombs along with the powder a powerfull subtile poison perfectly innocent untill ignited but deadly and awfully destructive when fired, poisoning the atmosphere for several rods in every direction. ...

> Isham Walker
> Jeff Davis Rifles
> 9th Regiment Miss. Volunteers

Warfare today allows generals to direct field operations miles away from the action. During the Civil War, however, commanders often led their men into battle. At Franklin, Tennessee, on November 30, 1864, the Confederate army suffered the loss of five generals in one skirmish.

In no other single battle have so many generals lost their lives.

The antipersonnel mine (booby trap) was first developed as a defensive weapon during the Civil War. It was conceived by Brigadier General Gabriel James Rains of the Confederate army. An expert on explosives, he perfected the mechanism that caused the mines to explode upon contact. They were hidden under dead soldiers or buried in the roads and caused heavy Union losses.

The weapon was attacked by Federals and Confederates alike. Confederate commander General Longstreet prohibited its use, declaring it an inhuman device. He described it as "not proper."

But by the end of the war, it had been accepted as legitimate and was employed by both sides.

The Civil War was the first major conflict in which the revolver was a primary weapon.

The Confederate army was the first officially to use the rapid-fire machine gun in battle. This gun was capable of firing 60 rounds per minute, a phenomenal rate at that time. However, the South soon discovered that lack of steel and manufacturing facilities curtailed its ability to mass-produce it.

The Northern army ordnance generals paid little attention to the machine gun until President Lincoln insisted that ten light models be purchased for testing. This model could fire at the rate of 120 rounds per minute.

A physician by the name of Richard Gatling perfected the gun so that it had a rapid-fire rate of 250 rounds per minute. It was not until after the war, however, that the United States army officially adopted the Gatling gun as a standard weapon.

The secret weapon that could have shortened the Civil War was demonstrated in front of Northern army ordnance officials as early as 1861. Unfortunately, these old-line officers lacked the vision to change established armaments. Not until 1863 was the Spencer repeating rifle officially adopted by the army. Soldiers had to wait, however, until 1864 for sufficient supplies to be manufactured and distributed.

The rapid-succession fire power of the rifle was an advantage of such proportions that it made the old standard muzzleloaders obsolete. One gun was the equivalent of five soldiers. The South had nothing to compare with it, and it lacked the facilities to manufacture it in quantity.

An obscure army officer, Colonel Wilder, recognized its potential and refused to stand idly by. He knew the weapon could be obtained privately from local manufacturers, so he personally purchased some for his entire brigade. With the gun's superior fire power, the men soon gained fame as the "Lightning Brigade."

The longest reported rifle shot of the war was measured at over one mile (5,467 feet). The rifle used to fire this shot was specially designed and equipped with a telescopic lens. It was estimated to have weighed between thirty and sixty pounds, and was mounted on a bench rest to steady it.

A Federal officer, Captain Medcalf, decided to use it to assassinate a Confederate general. Standing on a camouflaged hilltop with a pair of binoculars and a surveyor's transit, he accurately located the headquarters of the enemy garrison. He took into consideration the amount of the black powder load and the elevation of fire that would be necessary to get off an accurate shot. He also calculated that it would take five seconds for the bullet to reach its intended target.

When his chance came, the rifle was sighted and fired. An aide counted the seconds and the general fell dead at the count of five, a victim of one of the most remarkable rifle shots in history.

One of the popular devices introduced during the Civil War was the steel vest, or so-called bulletproof vest. It was not an official government issue. Civilian manufacturers produced thousands of them to sell to individual soldiers who wanted to protect themselves during battle. Because of their great weight, however, they were too cumbersome to wear and eventually were abandoned as impractical.

A few minutes past nine on the evening of February 17, 1864, a tremendous explosion in the harbor of Charleston, South Carolina, cut into the stillness of the evening. The blockading Federal sloop-of-war *Housatonic* slowly sank into a watery grave.

The watch on board ship could detect no enemy vessels in the vicinity. The Federal captain and crew did not know what had hit them. But it was soon learned that a new and ingenious Confederate warship, the CSS *H. L. Hunley*, had sunk the *Housatonic*. The *Hunley* was a submarine equipped with a torpedo, the first such vessel in naval history.

In 1861, the United States Army mustered into service 160 men to form the New York Rocket Battalion. They were to specialize in the use of newly designed rockets, expected to be more reliable and effective than their predecessors.

The new rockets failed their field tests so badly one army private commented that they "proved to be a fizzle." All that was left of the scheme was the battalion, which served as a unit under its original name for almost three years.

Ironically, the New York Rocket Battalion never fired a rocket.

In an early attempt at psychological warfare, the Union army, using aerial kites, dropped amnesty leaflets behind Confederate lines.

Aerial reconnaissance was first used during the Civil War. By means of inflated gas-filled balloons, both the North and South observed troop movements and directed field artillery to shell enemy positions accurately.

The first recorded antiaircraft fire occurred when artillery and snipers fired on these observation balloons.

A primitive version of an aircraft carrier was used to transport balloons to spy on enemy harbor fortifications. They were attached to flat riverboat barges which were then towed to strategic positions on open water, enabling observers to reconnoiter from the air.

The man who directed the Army Balloon Observation Corps for the North was a self-styled professor, Thaddeus Sobieski Constantine Lowe. He was employed by the army as a civilian expert on lighter-than-air craft and paid ten dollars a day. His official title, as registered on army records, was "Chief Aeronaut."

The first telegram ever sent from the air was transmitted to President Lincoln by a man in a balloon. In order to see if a message could be received, a cable was strung between the ground and a balloon stationed five hundred feet over Washington, D.C. The experiment was a success.

Two patents filed in 1862 describe with schematic drawings a rudimentary type of jet rocket aircraft and, of all things, a helicopter (patent no. 35453, filed by Arthur Kensella; and patent no. 35437, filed by L. C. Crowell).

Before the war, Jefferson Davis was secretary of war in the Cabinet of President James Buchanan. It was under his direction that one of the most remarkable United States Army experiments was undertaken.

Believing mules could not easily maneuver over rugged terrain or sustain themselves for long periods of time on forced marches, Davis imported a number of camels just before the war to take the mules' place on a trial basis. They were to be used as army pack animals in what are now the states of Texas, Arizona, New Mexico, Utah, Nevada and California.

The experiment was a failure, but offspring of "Uncle Sam's camels" were seen roaming the plains as late as 1948. To this day there is a law in Arizona making it illegal to hunt camels.

———————

For years after the Civil War, attention remained focused on the Southern prisoner-of-war camp known as Andersonville. By 1910, some one hundred fifty books and reviews detailing the horrors experienced by Northern prisoners of war had been circulated by Northern publishing houses. Yet while Andersonville claimed the lives of over thirteen thousand Federal prisoners, Northern prison camps were notoriously inadequate too.

Fort Delaware, a Northern camp established long before Andersonville, was located on Pea Patch Island in the Delaware River. It had been built to hold no more than four thousand prisoners, yet housed over twelve thousand. The prison was so poorly managed by Federal authorities that prisoners were forced to drink polluted river water to quench their thirst. This caused an epidemic of cholera that in one month alone killed over three hundred men. During 1863, the monthly death toll in the prison was over 12 percent of the total prisoner population. This was 3 percent higher than the most horrible figures reported at Andersonville. Poor rations, unsanitary conditions, insufficient supplies of medicine, a shortage of doctors and the brutality of prison guards were the most frequent causes of death.

One must not forget that this camp was located in the North, where supplies of rations were plentiful. The South could at least try to excuse its atrocities by pointing to the fact that as the war progressed it could not even supply shoes for its soldiers, much less rations for its prisoners.

———————

Camp Douglas, a Federal prison outside of Chicago, contained over thirty-eight hundred Confederate prisoners. In just one month, 10 percent of them died. Conditions at this camp were so intolerable that a United States sanitary commission, an early version of the Red Cross, recommended that the camp be evacuated. Instead, even more soldiers were confined there.

Camp Chase, Point Lookout, Elmira, Rock Island and Fort Johnson were also camps charged with inadequate facilities.

In 1866, official figures of prison mortality rates were made public by Secretary of War Stanton. They showed that of 270,000 Union soldiers captured by the Confederates, 22,500 died in prison, and of 220,000 Confederates captured by the Union, 26,400 died in prison. Therefore, of the deaths reported, a total of almost 9.3 percent were Southern prisoners of war, while only 8 percent were Northern prisoners of war.

———————

One of the worst reported incidents of Northern brutality to Southern prisoners of war was the "Yankee *Crescent* Hellship Cruise" in which six hundred Confederate officers were squeezed into the hold of a small steamship, the *Crescent*, in order to transport them to Charleston.

Conditions during the trip were awful. The room holding the men was directly behind the boiler room and the heat soon became unbearable. Three-fourths of them were forced to stand, and the heat and lack of available water combined to make most of them violently seasick. Vomit spewed forth at an uncontrollable rate; human waste covered the prisoners. The stench polluted the air from one end of the ship to the other.

At one point, the men went without water for over forty hours.

When it was finally supplied, they found it had been taken from the condensers and dispensed while still boiling.

Of the six hundred men who arrived at Charleston, only two hundred survived the next part of their journey, the trip to Fort Delaware.

———

VI

"All We Lack Is a Paler Hue"

"I am not in favor of making voters or jurors of Negroes, nor of qualifying them to hold office. . . . I am not in favor of Negro citizenship."

So spoke Abraham Lincoln in 1858, during one of his early political campaigns.

The first major clash between antislavery and proslavery forces took place at Harpers Ferry on October 16, 1859. John Brown unsuccessfully attempted to raid the Federal arsenal there.

Known as "Ole Osawatomie" Brown, he had in 1856 led the massacre at Osawatomie, Kansas, during which several men were tortured and murdered for their alleged proslavery activities. Brown was known to have strains of insanity running through his family. Seventeen relatives were insane, including two of his children, six of his first cousins, and nine members of his mother's family.

The Federal officer who was instrumental in his capture at Harpers Ferry was Colonel Robert E. Lee.

The first casualty of the raid was a free black bystander who was accidentally shot by Brown's men as he ran from the scene of the confrontation.

Witnessing the execution of John Brown on December 7, 1859, was a member of the Richmond Militia, John Wilkes Booth.

The permanent constitution of the Confederate States of America, adopted on March 11, 1861, abolished the African slave trade.

When the war broke out, some free Southern blacks pledged themselves to the Confederate cause partly because they were under pressure from whites to do so. For example, the free black community of New Orleans formed a military command known as the Native Guards. These men were "ready to take arms at a moment's notice and fight shoulder to shoulder with other Southern citizens." They later became part of the Confederate State Militia, working on labor battalions building fortifications and earthworks.

In the spring of 1862, when Federal forces captured New Orleans, the Native Guards refused to leave the city with the rest of the Confederate army. They were free at last to fight for the cause they believed in, and they welcomed the Federal army by swearing allegiance to the Union. Later, they joined the Union army and fought gallantly for the North the rest of the war.

The South, in desperate need of men for its dwindling army, considered the prospect of permitting the black man to shoulder arms and fight alongside the white soldier; but before the decision could be made, the war ended.

The first official regiment of volunteers consisting of Negro soldiers was the First South Carolina Volunteers, with Thomas Wentworth Higginson as its appointed white colonel.

The first Northern black regiment was the Fifty-fourth Massachusetts. Two sons of Frederick Douglass, the prominent black lecturer and author, were the first recruits from New York to join it.

The Congress of the United States actually purchased slaves for the purpose of setting them free. Before that, however, many solutions to the slavery problem in America had been proposed. Lincoln favored "compensated emancipation," and Congress passed a bill which he signed on April 16, 1862. It directed that loyal slave owners residing in the District of Columbia be compensated for their slaves in payments of sums not exceeding $300 for each slave freed. The bill authorized the United States Treasury to appropriate $1 million for this purpose.

As the war progressed, the problem of what to do with liberated slaves became a major issue. Lincoln strongly believed in the "colonizing abroad" of free black men. In an interview with five blacks on August 14, 1862, he said:

> Whether it is right or wrong I need not discuss, but this physical difference is a great disadvantage to us both, as I think yours suffer very greatly, many of them by living among us, while ours suffer from your presence.
>
> There is an unwillingness on the part of our people, harsh as it may be, for you free colored people to remain with us. I do not propose to discuss this, but to propose it as a fact with which we have to deal. I cannot alter it if I would. . . . It is better for us both, therefore, to be separated.

Liberia and Haiti offered freed slaves full citizenship, but prominent black leaders like Frederick Douglass opposed emigration. However, colonies were established; they met with failure.

The white labor force in the North was violently against the emancipation of blacks, seeing that as a threat to its earning capacity. Antiblack prejudice spread throughout several principal Northern cities, and between 1862 and 1863 turned into mob violence.

In August of 1862, a mob of laborers stormed a tobacco factory in Brooklyn which employed about twenty-five blacks. They set fire to the factory, but local police were able to save the women and children working there.

On March 6, 1863, several blacks were pulled from their homes and murdered when an angry white mob invaded the black district in Detroit. Thirty-two houses were destroyed and over two hundred people left homeless.

The bloodiest four days were the New York draft riots in 1863. Blacks were lynched and strung up on lampposts. Many more were murdered in their homes. A black orphanage was burned to the ground. The mob of white rioters was so large that police were helpless to stop them—they took refuge in local stationhouses. New York City was a battleground with streets barricaded and the mob in complete control. It was necessary to call troops in from Gettysburg to bring order to the city.

At the outbreak of the Civil War, the issue of permitting blacks to join the Union army was heatedly debated. Frederick Douglass fought against the notion that this conflict was a "white man's war" and that both citizenship and the right to fight could be denied to blacks. In 1861, he wrote: "Once let the black man get upon his person the brass letters, U.S., let him get an eagle on his button and a musket on his shoulder and bullets in his pocket and there is no power on earth which can deny that he has earned the right to citizenship in the United States."

In a speech at Cooper Union on February 12, 1862, he said: "Colored men were good enough to fight under Washington. They are not good enough to fight under McClellan. They were good enough to fight under Andrew Jackson. They are not good enough to fight under General Halleck. They were good enough to help win American independence but they are not good enough to help preserve that independence against treason and rebellion."

On July 17, 1862, Congress passed the necessary legislation permitting the black man to enlist in the Union army as a fighting soldier.

The black man's color made him subject to discriminatory pay allowances in the Union army. The white soldier received thirteen dollars a month with a clothing allowance of three fifty, the black soldier ten dollars a month with a three-dollar deduction for clothing.

A black corporal serving with the Fifty-fourth Massachusetts Regiment wrote an inspiring letter to President Lincoln appealing for equal pay for black soldiers.

> Camp of 54th Mass. Colored Regt.
> Morris Island, Dept. of the South
> Sept. 28th 1863

Your Excellency Abraham Lincoln:

Your Excellency will pardon the presumption of an humble individual like myself in addressing you but the earnest Solicitation of my Comrades in Arms besides the genuine interest felt by myself in the matter is my excuse for placing before the Executive head of the Nation our Common Grievances.

On the 6th of the last month, the Paymaster of the department informed us that if we would decide to receive the sum of $10. per month, he would come and pay us that sum, but that, on the sitting of Congress, the Regt. would, in his opinion be allowed the other 3. He did not give us any guarantee that this would be as he hoped. Certainly he had no authority for making any such guarantee and we cannot suppose him acting in any way interested.

Now the main question is are we Soldiers or are we Laboureres. We are fully armed and equipped, have done all the various Duties pertaining to a Soldiers life, have conducted ourselves to the complete satisfaction of General Officers, who were, if anything prejudiced against us, but who now accord us all the encouragement and honour due us; have shared the perils and Labour of reducing the first stronghold that flaunted a Traitor Flag and more, Mr. President.

Today, the Anglo-Saxon Mother, Wife, or sister are not alone in tears for departed Sons, Husbands and Brothers. The patient, trusting Descendants of Afric's Clime have dyed the ground with blood, in defense of the Union, and Democracy. Men, too, your Excellency, who know, in a measure, the cruelties of the Iron heel of oppression, which in years gone by, the very Power their blood is now being spilled to maintain, ever ground them to the dust.

But when the war trumpet sounded o'er the land, when men knew not the Friend from the Traitor, the Black man laid his life at the Altar of the nation—and he was refused. When the arms of the Union were beaten in the first years of the War and the Executive called more food for its ravaging maw, again the black man begged the privilege of Aiding his Country in her need, to be again refused.

And now he is in the War and how has he conducted himself? Let their dusky forms rise up out of the mires of James Island and give the answer. Let the rich mould around Wagner's parapets be upturned and there will be found an Eloquent answer. Obedient and patient and solid as a wall are they. All we lack is a paler hue and a better acquaintance with the Alphabet.

Now your Excellency, we have done a Soldier's Duty. Why can't we have a Soldier's pay? You caution the Rebel Chieftain that the United States knows no distinction in her Soldiers. She insists on having all her Soldiers, of whatever creed or Color to be treated according to the usages of War. Now if the United States exacts uniformity of treatment of her Soldiers from the insurgents, would it not be well and consistent to set the example herself by paying all her Soldiers alike? We of this Regt were not enlisted under any "contraband" act. But we do not wish to be understood as rating our Services of more Value to the Government than the service of the exslaves. This Service is undoubtedly worth much to the Nation but Congress made express provision touching their case as Slaves freed by Military necessity and assuming the Government to be their temporary Guardian.

Not so with us Freemen by birth and consequently, having the advantage of thinking and acting for ourselves, so far as the Laws would allow it. We do not consider ourselves fit subject for the Contraband Act.

We appeal to you, Sir, as the Executive of the Nation, to have us justly Dealt with. The Regt. do pray that they be assured their service will be fairly appreciated by paying them as American Soldiers, not as menial hirelings. Black men, you may well know, are poor. Three dollars per month for a year will supply their needy Wives and little ones with fuel. If you, as chief magistrate of the Nation, will assure us of our Whole pay. We are content; our Patriotism, our enthusiasm, will have a new impetus to exert our energy more and more to aid our Country.

Not that our hearts ever flagged in Devotion, spite the evident apathy displayed in our behalf, but we feel as though our Country spurned us now we are sworn to serve her.

Please give this a moment's attention.

Corporal James Henry Gooding
Co. C., 54th Mass. Regt

Corporal Gooding was wounded and taken prisoner. Confined to Andersonville Prison, he died just one month before Congress, in 1864, approved equal pay for black troops.

———————

Carrying the flag into battle was an honor and a duty entrusted only to the bravest soldier in a regiment. Loss or capture of the flag by the enemy resulted in demoralization and sometimes defeat. Battlefield descriptions of wounded color sergeants holding up the flag until an onrushing soldier could take it from his grasp and continue the charge were commonplace.

In 1863, during the Union assault on Fort Wagner, Sergeant William H. Carney defied bullets and artillery fire to race toward the color sergeant who had been shot and heroically snatched the colors from his hands before he went down. Continuing the assault and rallying his men with the flag, Sergeant Carney reached the parapet of the fort and placed the flag at the top for all to see and cheer. Although the assault was driven back, he made certain to carry off the colors, and in so doing, was wounded twice.

For his heroism, Sergeant Carney was awarded the Medal of Honor. He was the first black man ever to receive it.

———————

Confederate major general Nathan Bedford Forrest was referred to among blacks as "the Butcher of Fort Pillow." He earned this title by attacking the Union garrison at Fort Pillow on April 12, 1864, and instructing his command to give "no quarter" to the black Union soldiers who were defending the fort. So large was the number of black troops found slaughtered during the attack that the incident was termed "The Fort Pillow Massacre."

General Forrest is credited with originating the famous one-sentence principle for achieving victory: "The one who gets there first with the most is usually victorious."

Some three thousand Confederate kinfolk owe a debt of gratitude to an obscure cemetery caretaker by the name of John Jones, a fugitive slave from Virginia.

During the period of 1864 to 1865, the Union prison camp at Elmira, New York, held over twelve thousand Southern prisoners of war. As the death toll mounted due to disease and intense cold, Jones carefully noted the name, regiment, date of death and grave number of every victim. His efforts resulted in wooden markers identifying each grave so that relatives of the dead would know where they were buried.

Black troopers of the Fifth Massachusetts Cavalry were the first soldiers to enter Richmond after its evacuation of April 2-3, 1865.

Despite this and other instances of bravery, officers' commissions were continually denied to black soldiers. Eight surgeons were given medical commissions as majors, but, in all, not more than one hundred blacks (excluding chaplains) ever received commissions during the war.

By October 20, 1864, there were 140 black regiments in the

Union army, totaling 101,950 men. Fifteen of these regiments served in the Army of the Potomac during the massive invasion of Virginia in the summer of 1864. Black troops participated in every major Union campaign in 1864 and 1865 except Sherman's invasion of Georgia.

The Union navy took pride in the fact that one-fourth of its entire enlistment (approximately 29,000 men) consisted of blacks.

Approximately 186,000 black soldiers served in the Civil War, nearly 10 percent of the Union army. These men fought in 449 engagements of which 39 were major battles. Approximately 37,300 lost their lives. Seventeen soldiers and four sailors were awarded Congressional Medals of Honor.

The secret organization known as the Ku Klux Klan was established by a group of Confederate veterans in Pulaski, Tennessee, in December 1865. It was started strictly as a social club organized for the fraternal entertainment of ex-Confederate soldiers.

Frederick Douglass was the first Negro nominated as a candidate for President of the United States. At the Republican convention held in Chicago in 1888 he received one complimentary vote.

Notes

I. "The Prince of Ugly Fellows"

Page

1-5 Carl Sandburg, *Lincoln Collector* (New York: Bonanza Books, 1960), pp. 65-71.

5 Ruth Painter Randall, *Mary Lincoln* (New York: Dell Publishing, 1961), p. 431.

5 Ashley Halsey, Jr., *Who Fired The First Shot* (New York: Hawthorn Books, Inc., 1963), p. 93.

6 Randall, *Mary Lincoln,* pp. 54, 93, 97.

6 Joseph Nathan Kane, *Famous First Facts And Records* (New York: Ace Books, 1975 ed.), p. 478.

6-7 Philip Van Doren Stern, ed., *Prologue To Sumter* (New York: Fawcett Publications, Inc., 1961), pp. 363, 364, 377.

7 *New York Daily News,* April 8, 1973.

7 Stern, ed., *Prologue To Sumter,* p. 146.

7-8 Ibid., pp. 144, 308.

8 Randall, *Mary Lincoln,* pp. 321, 338, 361.

8 Ibid., p. 287.

8-9 Ibid., pp. 160, 310, 320.
Colonel John Wells Keeler, *Civil War Chronicle,* IV (New York: Oxford Publishing Co., 1971), p. 85.

9 Kane, *Famous First Facts,* p. 26.

9 Burke Davis, *Our Incredible Civil War* (New York: Holt, Rinehart and Winston, 1960), p. 151.

9 Kane, *Famous First Facts,* p. 43.

10 Davis, *Incredible Civil War,* p. 182.

10 Bertram W. Korn, *American Jewry and the Civil War* (New York: Meridian Books, 1961), p. 189.

10 George J. Olszewski, *Restoration of Fords Theatre* (Washington, D.C.: United States Department of the Interior, 1963), p. 105.

11   Lloyd Lewis, *Myths After Lincoln* (New York: The Readers Club, 1941), p. 160.

11   La Vere Anderson, "The Forgotten Lincoln," *Reader's Digest* (Reprinted from *Mankind* magazine, February 1969), pp. 172–78.

11-12   Lewis, *Myths After Lincoln*, pp. 152–53.

12   Harry Hansen, *The Civil War* (New York: Mentor Books, 1961), p. 548.

12   Randall, *Mary Lincoln*, p. 353.

12-14   Lewis, *Myths After Lincoln*, pp. 292–97.

14   Dorothy Meserve Kunhardt and Philip B. Kunhardt, Jr., *Twenty Days* (New York: Harper & Row, 1965), pp. 108, 197.

14-15   Ibid., pp. 95, 97, 99, 100, 101.

16   Kane, *Famous First Facts*, p. 477.

16   Kunhardt and Kunhardt, Jr., *Twenty Days*, p. 228.

16   John Cottrell, *Anatomy of An Assassination* (London: Frederick Muller, Ltd., 1966), p. 158.

16-17   Lewis, *Myths After Lincoln*, pp. 246–58.

17-18   Ibid., pp. 236–42.

18   Ibid., pp. 164–65, 180–81.

18-19   Ibid., pp. 206–9.

19-20   Ibid., pp. 222–25.

20-22   Otto Eisenschiml, *Why Was Lincoln Murdered?* (New York: Grosset & Dunlap, 1937), Chapters 1–29.
Cottrell, *Anatomy Of An Assassination*, p. 185.

22   Lewis, *Myths After Lincoln*, p. 51.

22-23   Ibid., pp. 261, 280–81, 288.
New York Times, February 13, 1972, p. 38.

23-24   James A. Rhodes and Dean Jauchius, *The Trial of Mary Todd Lincoln* (New York and Indianapolis: Bobbs-Merrill Co., 1959), p. 17.
Randall, *Mary Lincoln*, pp. 444, 446, 447, 479.

24   Ibid., pp. 427, 428.
Kane, *Famous First Facts*, p. 440.
New York Times, December 29, 1972, p. 10.

24   Lewis, *Myths After Lincoln*, p. 228.

25   Anderson, "Forgotten Lincoln," *Reader's Digest*, February, 1968.

25   Ralph Newman and E. B. Long, *The Civil War Digest* (New York: Grosset & Dunlap, 1960), p. 50.

25   *New York Daily News*, November 12, 1972, p. 3.

25-26   *New York Times*, June 9, 1974, p. 54.

26-27   Cottrell, *Anatomy Of An Assassination*, pp. 13–14.

27   *New York Daily News*, April 18, 1975, p. 2.

II.   Heroes and Battles, Money and Taxes

Page

29-30   Sylvia D. Hoffert, "The Brooks-Sumner Affair," *Civil War Times Illustrated* (magazine hereinafter abbreviated *CWTI*) 11, No. 6 (October 1972), pp. 35–40.

30–31 Stern, *Prologue To Sumter*, pp. 296–302.

32 *CWTI*, editors, 9, No. 6 (October 1970), pp. 20–21.

32 Hansen, *The Civil War*, pp. 273–74.

32–33 Ibid., p. 77.

33 Philip Van Doren Stern, ed., *Soldier Life* (New York: Fawcett Publications, Inc., 1961), p. 226.

33 Davis, *Incredible Civil War*, p. 19.

33–35 R. A. Lewis, M. D., "The Search," *CWTI*, 9, No. 4 (July 1970), p. 39.

35–36 James I. Robertson, Jr., *The Civil War* (Washington, D. C.: 1963), p. 9.

36 Newman and Long, *Civil War Digest*, p. 46.

36 Stern, ed., *Soldier Life*, pp. 279–80

36 Hansen, *The Civil War*, p. 62.

36–37 Grover Criswell and Herb Romerstein, *The Official Guide to Confederate Money and Civil War Tokens* (New York: H. C. Publishers, 1971), p. 93.

37 *New York Times*, March 8, 1974, p. 1 and September 29, 1974, p. 33.

37–38 Korn, *American Jewry and the Civil War*, p. 121.

39 Hansen, *The Civil War*, p. 277.

39 Davis, *Incredible Civil War*, p. 142.

39–40 Joseph P. Fried, "The Draft Riots," *CWTI*, 4, No. 5 (August 1965), pp. 4–5.

40 Hansen, *The Civil War*, pp. 470–75.

41 Charles J. Jordan, *"All About Santa Claus and How He Grew and Grew," Yankee* magazine (December 1973), p. 62.

41 Robert S. Holzman, Ph. D., "The Civil War Brought Our Income Tax" (The dispatch published by Civil War Round-Table of New York City, January 1972).
Paul Beers, *"Income Tax," CWTI*, 9, No. 1 (April 1970), p. 21.

42 Ralph G. Newman, *Lincoln For The Ages* (New York: Pyramid Books, 1964), pp. 217–18.

42–43 Davis, *Incredible Civil War*, pp. 198–205.

44 Henry E. Simmons, *A Concise Encyclopedia of the Civil War* (New York: A. S. Barnes & Co., Inc., 1965), pp. 62–63.

44 Ibid., pp. 63–64.

44–45 Davis, *Incredible Civil War*, p. 77.

45 Kane, *Famous First Facts*, p. 446.

45 Newman, *Lincoln For The Ages*, p. 253.

45–47 Frederick H. Dyer, *A Compendium of the War of the Rebellion* (New York and London: Thomas Yoseloff, 1959), 1, Introduction.

III. The Confederate States of America Are Alive and Well

49 Davis, *Incredible Civil War*, p. 225.

49–50 Arlie R. Slabaugh, *Confederate States Paper Money* (Racine, Wisc.: Whitman Publishing Co., 1958), pp. 4, 21, 48.

51 Philip Van Doren Stern, ed., *Soldier Life*, pp. 163–64.

51 Grover Criswell and Herb Romerstein, *Confederate Money and Civil War Tokens*, p. 93.

51 Davis, *Incredible Civil War*, p. 186.

51 Ibid., p. 187.

51–52 Simons, *Encyclopedia of the Civil War*, p. 72.

52 Kane, *Famous First Facts*, p. 477.

52 Alexander C. Niven, ed., *The Civil War Centennial Calendar—1861* (1960), p. 62.

53 Hansen, *The Civil War*, pp. 63, 67.

53 Douglas Southall Freeman, *R. E. Lee* (New York: Charles Scribner's Sons, 1934), 1, p. 92.

53 Ibid., p. 334.

53 Robertson, Jr., *The Civil War*, p. 55.

53 Simons, *Encyclopedia of the Civil War*, pp. 61, 140.

54 *New York Times*, July 23, 1975, p. 1.

55 Davis, *Incredible Civil War*, p. 210.

55 *Richmond Dispatch*, 1973.

55–56 Robertson, Jr., *The Civil War*, pp. 7–8.

56 Davis, *Incredible Civil War*, pp. 69–71.

56–57 Bell I. Wiley, "Life In The South," *CWTI*, 8, No. 9 (January 1970), p. 4.

57–59 *Playboy* magazine, October 1973, p. 155.

59–60 *CWTI*, editors, 9, No. 6 (October 1972), p. 29.

60 Hansen, *The Civil War*, pp. 76–77.

60–61 Ezra J. Warner, *Generals In Gray* (Baton Rouge: Louisiana State University Press, 1959), p. 13.

61 *New York Daily News*, June 2, 1974, p. 13.

61–62 Bell I. Wiley, "Confederate Exiles In Brazil," *CWTI*, 4, No. 9 (January 1977), pp. 22–32.

IV. "A Soldier Has a Hard Life"

Page

63 Freeman, *R. E. Lee*, 1, p. 363.

63–64 Robertson, Jr., *The Civil War*, pp. 35–36.

64 Ibid., p. 26.

64 Davis, *Incredible Civil War*, p. 218.

Boatner III, *The Civil War Dictionary*, p. 113.

64 "Odds & Ends," editors, *CWTI*, 4, No. 7 (November 1965), p. 39.

64–65 Hansen, *The Civil War*, p. 37.

65 Stern, ed., *Prologue To Sumter*, pp. 349–50.

65 Warner, *Generals In Gray*, p. 282.

65 Ibid., preface.

65–66 Kane, *Famous First Facts*, p. 163.

66   Ibid., p. 164.
66   Davis, *Incredible Civil War*, pp. 63–64.
      Francis A. Lord and Arthur Wise, *Bands & Drummer Boys of the Civil War* (New York and London: Thomas Yoseloff, 1966), p. 107.
66   Joseph B. Mitchell, *The Badge of Gallantry* (New York: The Macmillan Co., 1968), p. 96.
66–67 Ibid., p. 97.
67   Warner, *Generals In Gray*, preface, p. xxvi.
67   *CWTI*, editors, 12, No. 4 (July 1973), p. 33.
67–68 G. Wayne King, "Death Camp at Florence," *CWTI*, 12, No. 9 (January 1974), p. 38.
68   Simons, *Encyclopedia of the Civil War*, p. 46.
68   *CWTI*, editors, 12, No. 4 (July 1973), p. 13.
68   Davis, *Incredible Civil War*, p. 221.
68   Warner, *Generals In Gray*, p. 92.
      Glenn Tucker, "Untutored Genius of the Civil War," *CWTI*, 6, No. 5 (August 1967), p. 38.
69   Robertson, Jr., *The Civil War*, p. 38.
69   Colonel Roy J. Honeywell, "Men of God," *CWTI*, 6, No. 5 (August 1967), p. 38.
69   E. M. Boswell, "Rebel Religion," *CWTI*, 9, No. 6 (October 1972), p. 30.
69   Ibid., p. 31.
69–70 Hansen, *The Civil War*, p. 107.
70   Davis, *Incredible Civil War*, p. 178.
70   Hansen, *The Civil War*, pp. 116–19.
71   Freeman, *R. E. Lee*, 1, p. 2.
71   Davis, *Incredible Civil War*, pp. 12, 96.
      Boatner III, *The Civil War Dictionary*, p. 322.
71–72 Robert Denning Clark, "From Union Army Volunteer to President," *CWTI*, 2, No. 10 (February 1969), p. 39.
72   Robertson, Jr., *The Civil War*, p. 38.
72   Davis, *Incredible Civil War*, p. 25.
72   Ibid., p. 222.
72–73 Ibid., pp. 76–77.
      Boatner III, *Civil War Dictionary*, p. 349.
73   Davis, *Incredible Civil War*, p. 142.
73   Boatner III, *The Civil War Dictionary*, p. 216.
73   Davis, *Incredible Civil War*, p. 159.
73–74 Ibid., pp. 162–63.
74   Hansen, *The Civil War*, p. 278.
74   Editors, "A Free Wheeler," *CWTI*, 1, No. 4 (July 1962), p. 45.
74   Hannah Campbell, *Why Did They Name It?* (New Yorᵏ: Fleet Publishing, 1964), p. 63.

75   Davis, *Incredible Civil War,* pp. 75–76.
75   Simons, *Encyclopedia of the Civil War,* pp. 165, 201.
75   Davis, *Incredible Civil War,* p. 94.
75   Simons, *Encyclopedia of the Civil War,* p. 64.
76–77 *New York Daily News Magazine,* December 10, 1972, p. 42.
     Irwin Richman, "Pauline Cushman," *CWTI,* 7, No. 10 (February 1969), p. 39.
77–80 Terry E. Baldwin, "Clerk of the Dead," *CWTI,* 9, No. 6 (October 1971), p. 12.
80–81 Hansen, *The Civil War,* pp. 165–68.
81   Editors, "General Schimmelfennigs Headquarters," *CWTI,* 9, No. 10 (February 1972), p. 18.
81   Newman and Long, *The Civil War Digest,* p. 48.
81   Mitchell, *Badge of Gallantry,* p. 4.
81–82 Ibid., pp. 10–12.
82   Davis, *Incredible Civil War,* p. 66.
     Mitchell, *Badge of Gallantry,* pp. 22, 96.
82–83 Halsey, Jr., *Fired the First Shot,* pp. 82–91.
83   Simons, *Encyclopedia of the Civil War,* pp. 72–73.
83–84 Stephen E. Ambrose, "The War Comes To West Point," *CWTI,* 4, No. 5 (August 1965), p. 32.
84   Halsey, Jr., *Fired the First Shot,* pp. 191–92.
84   Ibid., pp. 193–202.
85   Ibid., p. 182.
85   Ibid., pp. 183–184.
85   Davis, *Incredible Civil War,* p. 29.
85–86 Halsey, Jr., *Fired the First Shot,* p. 204.
86   Hansen, *The Civil War,* pp. 155–56.
86–87 Simons, *Encyclopedia of the Civil War,* p. 19.
87–88 Ibid., p. 100.
88   James I. Roberson, "Military Executions," *CWTI,* 5, No. 2 (May 1966), p. 36.
88   Korn, *American Jewry & the Civil War,* pp. 109–12.
88–89 Halsey, Jr., *Fired the First Shot,* p. 171.
89   Stern, ed., *Soldier Life,* p. 40.
89   Halsey, Jr., *Fired the First Shot,* pp. 61–66.
89   Stern, ed., *Soldier Life,* p. 147.
89–90 Ibid., introduction, p. viii.
90   Ibid., pp. 180–83.
90   Colonel John Wells Keeler, "Civil War Chronicle," August 1962, p. 36.
90   Stern, ed., *Soldier Life,* p. 28.
90–91 Ibid., p. 231.
91   Criswell and Romerstein, *Guide to Confederate Money,* p. 117.

91   E. M. Boswell, "Rebel Religion," *CWTI*, 11, No. 6 (October 1972), p. 28.

92   Stern, ed., *Soldier Life*, p. 79.

92   Ibid., p. 236.

92-93   Editor, "Spirited and Spicy," *CWTI*, 11, No. 9 (January 1973), pp. 26-27.

93   *New York Post*, November 1, 1972.

93-94   Byron Stinson, "Paying the Debt," *CWTI*, 9, No. 4 (July 1970), p. 29.

94   Lewis, *Myths After Lincoln*, p. 308.

94   *New York Daily News*, August 17, 1975.

94   Kane, *Famous First Facts*, p. 387.

94-95   From a taped interview by the author, January 9, 1972 in Winsted, Connecticut.

V.   "Beans Killed More Than Bullets"

Page

97-98   George Worthington Adams, *Doctors In Blue* (New York: H. Schuman, 1952), pp. 11, 12, 18, 21, 22.
William H. Prince, *The Civil War Centennial Handbook* (Arlington, Virginia: Prince Lithograph Co., 1961), p. 13.

98   Halsey, Jr., *Fired the First Shot*, p. 173.

98-99   Adams, *Doctors In Blue*, p. 123.

99   Ibid., pp. 102, 106, 111.

99-100   Ibid., p. 131.

100   Stern, ed., *Soldier Life*, p. 221.

100   Adams, *Doctors In Blue*, p. 50.

100   Halsey, Jr., *Fired the First Shot*, p. 174.

101   Adams, *Doctors In Blue*, p. 123.

101   Ibid., p. 102, 106.

101   Robertson, Jr., *The Civil War*, p. 60.

101   Adams, *Doctors In Blue*, p. 123.

102-3   Ibid., p. 108.

103   Ibid., p. 115.

103-4   Peter T. Harstad, "Draft Dodgers and Bounty Jumpers," *CWTI*, 6, No. 2 (May 1967), pp. 28-36.

104   Halsey, Jr., *Fired the First Shot*, pp. 176-77.

105   Ibid., p. 177.

105   Adams, *Doctors In Blue*, p. 131.

105-6   Ibid., p. 10.

106   Ibid., p. 64.

106-7   Davis, *Incredible Civil War*, p. 27.

107-8   *New York Daily News*, March 2, 1976, p. 38.

108-9   David B. Sabine, "Captain Sally Tompkins," *CWTI*, 4, No. 7 (November 1965), p. 36.

109   Halsey, Jr., *Fired the First Shot*, p. 178.

109-10   Adams, *Doctors In Blue*, pp. 153-55.

110   Davis, *Incredible Civil War*, p. 77.

110   Halsey, Jr., *Fired the First Shot*, p. 179.

110   Ibid., p. 179.

111-12   Dr. Harry J. Warthen, "Some Were Mighty Hard to Kill," *CWTI*, 2, No. 9 (January 1964), p. 19.

112   Glenn Tucker, "Curious Wounds at Chickamauga," *CWTI*, 8, No. 2 (May 1969), p. 46.

112-14   Dr. F. Donald Napolitani, *The Case of the Miraculous Bullet* (New York: American Heritage Publishing Co., 1971), p. 99.

114   Bell I. Wiley, "Drop Poison Gas From A Balloon," *CWTI*, 7, No. 4 (July 1968), p. 40.

114   Ibid., pp. 10-15

115   Colonel Campbell Brown, "Myth of the Five Dead Generals," *CWTI*, 8, No. 5 (August 1969), p. 14.

115   Warner, *Generals In Gray*, p. 31.

115   Halsey, Jr., *Fired the First Shot*, p. 67.

115-16   Ibid., pp. 71-73.

116   Ibid., pp. 65-68.

116-17   Ibid., pp. 117-18.

117   Stern, ed., *Soldier Life*, p. 195.

117   Davis, *Incredible Civil War*, p. 174.

117   Frank H. Winter and Mitchell R. Sharpe, "Major Lion's Rocketeers," *CWTI*, 11, No. 9 (January 1973), pp. 10-15.

118   Davis, *Incredible Civil War*, p. 31.

118   Halsey, Jr., *Fired the First Shot*, pp. 77-81.

118   Ibid., p. 80.

118   Ibid., p. 77.

119   Odie B. Falk, *The U. S. Camel Corps* (New York: Oxford University Press, 1976), p. 24.

119-20   Halsey, *Fired the First Shot*, pp. 143-48.

120   Ibid., pp. 146-47.

120-21   Ibid., p. 161.

VI.   "All We Lack Is a Paler Hue"

Page

123   Hansen, *The Civil War*, p. 30.

123-24   Davis, *Incredible Civil War*, p. 84.

Simons, *Encyclopedia of the Civil War*, pp. 41-42, 103-4.

124   Hansen, *The Civil War,* p. 35.

124   James M. McPherson, *The Negro's Civil War* (New York: Vintage Books, 1967), p. 23.

124–25   Ibid., pp. 165, 173, 176.

125   Ibid., pp. 89–91.

Hansen, *The Civil War,* pp. 268, 270.

125–26   McPherson, *Negro's Civil War,* pp. 70–71.

126   Ibid., p. 161–63.

127   Ibid., p. 165.

127–29   Editors, "Are We Soldiers or Are We Labourers?" *CWTI,* 11, No. 1 (April 1972), pp. 38–39.

129   Mitchell, *Badge of Gallantry,* pp. 132–34.

129–30   Simons, *Encyclopedia of the Civil War,* p. 82.

Halsey, Jr., *Fired the First Shot,* p. 54.

130   Editors, "Negro Friends of Rebel Dead," *CWTI,* 5, No. 7 (November 1966), p. 49.

130   McPherson, *Negro's Civil War,* pp. 158, 223.

130–31   Ibid., p. 237.

131   V. C. Jones, "The Rise and Fall of the Ku Klux Klan," *CWTI,* 2, No. 10 (February 1964), p. 12.

131   Kane, *First Facts and Records,* p. 479.

Index

143